Misbehavin' Monarchs

D1600360

MISBEHAVIN' MONARCHS

Exploring Biblical Rulers of Questionable Character

BARBARA J. ESSEX

THE PILGRIM PRESS • CLEVELAND

This work is lovingly dedicated to my nieces, nephews, and godchildren:

Ta-Tanisha, Eddie Jr., Nathan Jr., Norell, Shondale, Alyssa, Sade, Ta-Tiairra, D'Myreo, Julius, Dawn, Robin, and Kwame.

MAY PEACE, JOY, AND POWER BE YOUR COMPANIONS!

The Pilgrim Press, 700 Prospect Avenue, Cleveland, Ohio 44115,
thepilgrimpress.com
© 2006 by Barbara Essex

Printed in the United States of America on acid-free paper

10   09   08   07   06   5   4   3   2   1

Library of Congress Cataloging-in-Publication Data

Essex, Barbara J. (Barbara Jean), 1951–
    Misbehavin' monarchs : exploring Biblical kings of questionable character /
Barbara J. Essex.
        p.   cm.
    ISBN-13: 978-0-8298-1655-6 (alk. paper)
    1. Kings and rulers—Biblical teaching.   2. Bible. O.T. Kings—Textbooks.
3. Bible. O.T. Chronicles—Textbooks.   I. Title.

BS1199.K5E87   2006
221.9'22—dc22   2006026528

ISBN-13: 978-0-8298-1655-6
ISBN-10: 0-8298-1655-0

CONTENTS

GETTING STARTED

This is a ten-week study of biblical rulers for individual and/or group study. If used for group study, leaders do not need extensive small group training. The study begins with some thoughts on leadership. Each study unit reviews the stories of selected biblical rulers and ends with reflection questions to help start a discussion about what we can learn from these characters and their stories. This book is designed to help us examine issues of leadership and identity as well as the motives and assumptions we bring to our work and ministry.

Each study session needs about two hours; feel free, however, to make adjustments that work for you or your group. The materials you need include this book, a Bible version with which you are comfortable, and a notebook or journal in which to record your answers to the questions and your reflections on the lessons.

Each study unit follows the same pattern:

- A review of the selected leader's story
- Additional information to help make the story accessible and understandable
- A set of reflection questions

You may want to follow the suggested format:

- Assign readings ahead of time—the scripture as well as the unit to be studied.
- If necessary, set some "ground rules" for the discussion (for example, everyone will have an opportunity to voice his/her opinion without judgment from other group members; no one needs to agree with everyone else; no name calling; etc.).
- Begin each session with a prayer; ask God for open minds and meaningful discussion.
- Review the information in the study unit; answer any questions.
- Use the reflection questions at the end of each unit to start the discussion.
- Share insights about the text and as much as people feel comfortable with sharing.
- Assign the next unit.
- Close with prayer, thanking God for fruitful conversation and for God's help in preparing for the next session.

If you are using this resource for personal study, you should allot one and a half to two hours for each study unit. You will need a journal in which to record your reflections and questions.

At the end of this book, you will find a section with themes to consider for preaching and teaching about biblical kings (and a queen). The teaching section suggests ways to help persons enter the stories. The preaching section lifts up theological themes found in the stories. Finally, there is a resources section for those who wish to continue their study of biblical monarchs. Of course, you should include any resources you find helpful to supplement the lessons here.

I hope you will find creative ways to make these studies fun and informative. There are no hard and fast rules about how to study these characters—they are human and we have an opportunity to see just how human they are—with their fine points and flaws. There is much we can learn from these biblical folks as well as about ourselves. I hope that these study units will help deepen your faith and broaden your service towards others. I hope you find this study to be informative, challenging and inspirational. I pray God will bless you as you journey deeper into God's Word.

ACKNOWLEDGMENTS

Writing is a solitary activity. For weeks on end, writers have to isolate themselves in order to focus and to get the work done. This means family and friends are put on hold during the writing; it helps the writer when they are paragons of patience and understanding. I am grateful to my support system—Patricia, Sheri, Ta-Tanisha, Christine, Gregory, Eddie, Linda, Quinn, Ann, Belinda, Edward, O'Weedy, LaVerne, Gayle, Johari, Roland, Marjorie —for loving me in spite of unreturned phone calls, too brief e-mail messages, missed dinners and movies, and ignored shopping invitations. I love y'all madly.

I am grateful to Kim Martin Sadler, who always spurs me on with her support and tough love. I am grateful, also, for the support of Michael Lawrence and the folks at The Pilgrim Press who work hard to get my words out.

And a special thank-you to members of congregations across the world who wrestle with me to make sense of the Bible—your prayers make my work easier.

As always, any strength of this work is due to the constructive feedback of my conversation partners; all weaknesses are due to my own inadequacies.

INTRODUCTION

We have looked at some of the bad girls, bad boys, and dysfunctional families of the Bible. What fun we've had exploring their stories. And there are even more stories to tell. When the people of Israel ask for a ruler, we see a major shift in the biblical story. The time of God's rule gives way to the personalities who assume leadership of the people. The stories of Israel's rulers make fascinating case studies for leadership issues and concerns. We will trace the ups and downs of their reigns in *Misbehavin' Monarchs*.

We will evaluate their leadership—what they did well, where they fell short, and what we can learn from them. We will watch them deal with political, social, religious, and personal crises. We will explore their stories by looking at their character and personality, their strengths and weaknesses, their defining moments of leadership, the consequences of their decisions and choices, and their legacy for future generations.

The books of Samuel, Kings, and Chronicles introduce us to some of the big personalities in the Bible: Hannah, Samuel, Saul, David, Solomon, Elijah, Jezebel, and Elisha. When the nation is divided after Solomon's reign, some are marginally known and recognized. We may recall the stories, in Judah, of Asa, Jehoshaphat, Uzziah, Hezekiah, and Josiah. We may recall the stories, in Israel, of Ahab and Jehu. Others in both the Northern and Southern territories are relatively unknown to us: Athaliah, Ahaz, Manasseh, Zedekiah, Jeroboam, Zimri, Jeroboam II, Hoshea. We find in these stories of biblical monarchs the rise of the prophetic office as a counterpoint to the rulership. We watch Israel during its transition from tribal life to centralized nation—a transition that was not easy and did little to overcome the friction that was always a part of Israel's life. There are times when rulers and prophets seem like team players and other times when the tension between the two is unbearable. We witness the decline and ultimate destruction of Israel as a nation at the hands of the Babylonians and Assyrians. We watch the people experience their greatest fears—exile from the land God has promised them *and* estrangement from their God. Each has a story to contribute to our understanding of our faith tradition.

The leadership of these rulers in the Hebrew Bible forms part of the foundation upon which our Christian tradition rests. When we encounter phrases like "the territory of God," "the City of David," and "ruler of the Jews," political, social, and theological statements are being made that have their roots in the period of the monarchy. We cannot fully understand what these terms mean unless we understand the back story that gives rise to them. *Misbehavin' Monarchs* will attempt to fill in that gap.

The story of God's dealings with God's people marches through history with a number of twists and turns. God's call to Moses is filled with magic, intrigue, danger, and triumph. It is filled, too, with false starts, backward steps, and unfulfilled hopes. Before Moses dies, he passes the baton to Joshua, who moves the people into the land promised by God.

The people are caught off guard at the difficulty of settling into the land. After a series of battles, at long last the people are settling in the promised land and living into their covenant with the God who is their deliverer and sustainer. The story of Jacob is prominent and sets the stage for this period in Israel's life. After his death, Jacob's legacy lives on in the "twelve tribes" of Israel.

The tribes, which parallel the sons of Jacob (with Joseph's share divided between his two sons, Ephraim and Manasseh), live in their territories and get along fairly well, though with the occasional flare-up among the tribes. The tribes see themselves as family and are held together by the memory of God's deliverance from slavery in Egypt and by God's covenant with them.

The Exodus from Egypt creates a new people, Israel. God chooses to free them and chooses to be in intimate relationship with them. The people agree to be obedient to God's will and commandments. Israel is established and held together by God's actions and not by formal structures of government. The people's theological understanding and lived experience of God form the center that holds the tribes together.

Throughout Israel's history, God reminds them that they have been chosen, protected, and empowered for a purpose: to be an example to other nations that there is life, community, and well-being in living under God's divine rule. This is a purpose that Israel often forgets and ignores. The glue that holds the tribal league together is their belief, faith, and trust in God, who is ever on their side. In other words, Israel's true leader is God, YHWH, the God of Abraham, Isaac, and Jacob. God regularly calls upon persons to perform specific tasks, but the ultimate leader for Israel is God.

As we look at the rulers of Israel, we will find our own stories embedded in their stories. We will look at circumstances of war and violence. We will explore personality quirks and the results of those idiosyncrasies. We will look at how leaders are influenced by those who surround them. We will laugh at the foibles of leaders and cry when those characteristics have tragic consequences for innocent people.

This volume is a continuation of my work to make the Bible fun and accessible while challenging us to think about our own lives, work, ministry, and leadership. *Misbehavin' Monarchs* seeks to present an informed, critical picture of biblical characters and issues. We will be drawing on scholarship from various methods for reading and interpreting biblical texts.

There is much to consider as we look at the rulers of Israel—some of the stories are gruesome and some are funny—all of them have something to say to us today. As we reflect on our own leadership concerns, we can draw on the wisdom we find in the Bible. We will explore stories that teach us what to do and what not to do. I hope you will laugh and cry as you study this portion of our faith tradition and that you will leave the study knowing more about the Bible and yourself than before you started this study.

Shalom!

PART ONE

THE UNITED TERRITORY
All Israel

We are about to enter a different world—a world of politics, intrigue, and brutality. Israel had three tasks to face:

- To settle into the land God had promised to its ancestors
- To resist the efforts of other nations that tried to conquer Israel or resisted being displaced by Israel
- To remain faithful and obedient to the one God, YHWH

Any one of these tasks would be daunting; but the three together almost feel like a set-up. The tasks required strong and focused leadership—something Israel sorely needed. It was no easy thing to settle into Palestine—mostly because people were already settled there and occupying the land. The "Canaanites" were various groups of people who were indigenous to the land as well as folks migrating to the area like Israel. During ancient times, large groups of people were on the move and for a number of reasons—floods, droughts, famine, and political, social, and economic upheaval, among others. All were looking for a space where they could live and thrive. So, Israel found itself part of a large demographical shift.

In addition to trying to displace folks who were there first, Israel also had to deal with folks who wanted more land than they needed even though the land was occupied. The area that Israel claimed had some advantages—water, trade and travel routes, grazing and farming land—and if Israel wanted the land, so did other nations. Those other nations were often more organized and armed to complete their takeovers. The other nations or city-states were ruled by rulers who provided the leadership needed to be powerhouses in the region. The rulers were able to mobilize their people and troops to get the job done—make a name for themselves by conquering other peoples and taking their land. So we are not surprised to read story after story about wars—past wars, current wars, and impending wars. This part of Israel's history is focused on defensive and offensive moves as it vies for its own space to live, survive, and thrive.

To make matters even more challenging, Israel was different from the other peoples in the area. Israel worshiped only one God, YHWH. Israel's God, like other gods, was a warrior—fighting for and on behalf of Israel. However, Israel's God was not interested in serving alongside other gods. Israel's God was and is a jealous God who had strict rules for the people. At least, that's the view of the writers of this part of the Bible!

It would be nice if Israel had videotaped or kept a running chronicle of its experiences. What we have instead are some of the most confusing and disturbing passages of scripture. These books are filled with names and places that make little sense to us. Different people in the Bible have the same name and it is difficult to figure out who's who. Names of cities and other places seem arbitrary and it is not easy to match places with people. And because we are not familiar with the geography, we have no idea how places are related to each other or why the place is important to the action in the story. If that's not enough, the stories themselves are confusing, repetitive, and contradictory. For instance, when did Saul actually meet David? One story indicates that Saul met David during a battle with the Philistines. Another story has David as the warrior musician in Saul's court. And there's more—this period in Israel's life is one of the bloodiest and goriest in the Bible. There is nothing but war, war, war in these texts. The people are commanded by God to utterly destroy cities—burning men, women, and children. God punishes those who do not carry out the command to wipe out people, places, and things. Determining the accuracy of the stories is what keeps scholars busy as they continue the work of separating truth from fiction.

We have quite human portraits of our ancestors in the faith. Samuel, the transition figure between the old tribal way and the new monarchy, is stern, mean, and passive-aggressive. Saul, the first ruler, is shown to be both competent and mentally ill. David, Israel's ideal ruler and warrior, rapes a married woman and kills her husband to cover up his indiscretion. He is unable to control his own family and watches as his family life deteriorates into violence and death. Solomon seems to have a sexual addiction but stops at nothing to build a fitting temple to God.

Women play significant roles in this part of Israel's story. The plight of Hannah sets the stage for the monarchy. Her actions symbolize the plight of Israel and God's responses to her and Israel set the stage for one of the greatest dramas in history. The drama surrounding Bathsheba shapes the royal life that David hides from as his children betray the purpose of family. In these books, we find the admonition against marrying foreign women—Jezebel is made the poster child for the outcome of such liaisons.

You will remember from other Bible studies that the Bible is composed of a number of traditions, each with a particular viewpoint and agenda. The work of scholars includes trying to identify the various strands of tradition and seeing how those strands are woven together to make up the Bible we have today. The "problem" with the Bible is that it is not history, not as we define history today.

The Bible was not written to be "objective," with facts and dates and places checked and double-checked for accuracy. The Bible is written against the backdrop of a people seeking to live into a reality marked by miraculous events—it is a message of God's dealings with humankind.

The Bible is more like divine drama than history. The stories are shaped by the purposes and perspectives of diverse persons who try to make sense out of the events of the day. The same stories are interpreted and reinterpreted as time goes on and are nuanced according to the needs of the people at any given time. The events themselves don't change, but how they are understood do. How one sees any event or situation is colored by one's context—age, gender, race, class, geographical location, and understanding of the world. This is true for biblical writers and editors of the traditions that we find in the Bible.

Scholars generally agree that a Deuteronomic-Deuteronomistic Historical (designated with the abbreviation Dtr or simply D) perspective shapes the treatment of the monarchy in Israel's story. The D tradition is found mainly in the book of Deuteronomy, with heavy influence seen in the books of Judges through 2 Kings. The tradition has strong ties and loyalty to the law of Moses and emphasizes the covenantal relationship between God and humankind. Its message is to encourage or urge Israelites to good deeds and to absolute loyalty to God as set forth in the Mosaic law.

This tradition is not so much interested in writing history. The D tradition is less interested in facts, figures, and historical accuracy. Rather, D seeks to judge whether the people adhere to God's teachings and covenant. In fact, rulers are judged primarily on their ability to walk in the ways of YHWH—rulers who do so are judged positively; those who fail are condemned as evil or wicked.

The stories about rulers are found in 1 and 2 Samuel and 1 and 2 Kings with supplementary material in 1 and 2 Chronicles. The stories of Israel's rulers include an evaluation of their leadership based on how well or poorly the ruler encouraged centralized worship at Jerusalem and how well the monarch followed God's commandments. Individual rulers are introduced in various ways that include dating a ruler's reign in relation to other rulers, where the ruler lives, the length of the ruler's reign, the age of the ruler when he took the throne, where the ruler was to be buried, and/or the name of his successor.

The stories are told from the perspective that values the old covenantal theology that states that Israel's destruction is due to the people turning away from God to other gods as well as belief in the promise given to David that his lineage would always be in power. The language of the Deuteronomistic historian reflects a period of religious crisis. Scholars believe the books received their final form during the collapse of Israel when the Assyrian threat to Judah continued and a number of evil rulers endangered YHWH religion. D believes that salvation could be had by a loyal response to YHWH's covenant laws and by returning to pure worship of God at Jerusalem.

The basic theme of D is that the judgment of Israel is due to the serious sins of the people. It is important for suffering people to have some sense about why they are suffering. In this case, the judgment of exile is justified and explained to the people so they would change their ways and return to obedience to God's law. At the heart of the stories is the continuing hope that God would reverse the situation and restore Israel to its former greatness. So, while the prophets admonish the rulers, they always hold out the possibility that ruler and people will get back on track and renew their covenant with God. We will see some efforts at reform in our study of Israel's rulers, but the people are either unwilling or unable to stay connected to God so that the covenantal promises are honored.

The theology behind D required total allegiance to and faith in the one God. If the people, including the rulers, did this, then YHWH watched over, protected, and brought prosperity to Israel. The belief of that time was that God controlled everything. Israel had experienced the one God as creator, sustainer, comforter, liberator, and judge. Israel's God heard the cries of the people, was moved with compassion, and actively worked on Israel's behalf. When the people were slaves in Egypt, YHWH rescued and delivered them. When the people were hungry and thirsty in the wilderness, YHWH provided manna and water. When the people were intimidated by the "giants" already occupying the promised land, YHWH raised up military leaders and gave them marching orders, and Israel prevailed.

One would think that a small nation like Israel would already have a strong ruler, a standing army, and a shed house of fine weapons. But Israel had none of those things. Israel was made up of twelve tribes that shared a common experience of YHWH; each tribe was like a tiny territory unto itself. Elders settled disputes, priests administered religious life, and YHWH held the tribes together. Whenever a tribe was in trouble, the other tribes helped out.

A question: how was that working for Israel? For a while, the tribal system worked well. But it became obvious that such a system would not last in the long run as the surrounding situation of war intensified. When other nations saw that Israel had no ruler and no centralized administration, they thought poor little Israel would be a pushover. And if that wasn't enough, the tribes had issues among themselves. They fought and squabbled about various things—whose territory was bigger, who followed YHWH more loyally, who offended whom, who played too closely with the enemies, who took too long to send support—there was always some kind of drama going on within Israel.

So, Israel was shaky internally and externally. It sought unity and community among the tribes at the same time it tried to hold off other nations. What to do? What to do?

A group of elders felt that they had had enough and had a solution—they wanted a ruler! In their minds, a ruler would put Israel on equal footing with other nations. Instead of waiting for YHWH to identify and equip a suitable leader, Israel would have someone who would take charge right away. Besides, the leaders YHWH had picked were increasingly problematic—Jephthah, Samson—need we say more?

The elders' request marked a huge paradigm shift for Israel. To our eyes, the request doesn't seem like a big deal. The desire for a ruler seems logical and reasonable. We may marvel at how well Israel had done without a ruler, but things had changed and Israel needed to change too. If the other nations had rulers, Israel should have one, too. Of course, this raises the age-old parental question: If the other nations jump off a cliff, will you jump, too?

The request for a ruler is a serious one. It doesn't just imply dissatisfaction with the current state of affairs; it marks a change in the people's attitude, thoughts, values, beliefs, and behavior towards God, the jealous God who must have absolute control and power. The elders imply that human power is better than divine power. And the stage is set for some interesting stories about big changes in Israel.

THE RULERSHIP THING: DEALING WITH A CHANGED REALITY

As we know, Israel was organized according to tribes that corresponded to the sons of Jacob. The tribes settled into the land promised by God, each in its respective region. The tribes rallied to help each other, as needed, against local and outside threats. The period after Joshua's leadership is called the time of the "judges" and forms a fairly predictable cycle of relative peace, idolatry, judgment, cries to God for help, God's raising up of a savior figure, leadership of the judge, and a time of peace. But the Book of Judges ends on an ominous note:

> *In those days there was no ruler in Israel; all the people did what was right in their own eyes.* (*Judg.* 21:25)

The people had shown throughout their history that they could not be trusted to remember and live out God's purpose for them. The very pattern of the age of the judges shows that they would turn away from God time and time again. After the last judge, Samson, died, a new kind of leader emerged. The need for a different leader emerged as Israel faced its most formidable opposition to date—the dreaded Philistines!

The Bible paints an unflattering picture of the Philistines. They are portrayed as a warring people—aggressive, disciplined, trained, and well-armed soldiers; superior weapons of iron, a fleet of chariots; and a central government that had plans to control all of western Palestine. Compared to them, the unorganized, ill equipped, squabbling tribes of Israel looked incompetent and helpless.

In a decisive battle, Israel was exposed as a weakling among the nations. The Philistines soundly and effectively attacked Israel and took away their weapons. The Philistines destroyed the religious center at Shiloh and took control of the ark of God, the portable shrine in which the physical manifestation of God's presence resided. Israel was in disarray, fearful, and scattered.

Samuel was able to rally the tribes to fight against the Philistines. Under his leadership, they recaptured the ark. Samuel served as a bridge between the old ways—the call of a charismatic military and judicial leader—and the beginnings of the new—a leader who would bring national and religious stability.

Samuel worked as priest and politician—he anointed and rejected rulers, interceded with God on behalf of the people, and guided the conscience and decisions of the people. Samuel embodied the last of what was good about the judges and the beginnings of the prophets who would work with rulers to hold them accountable to God. The people became concerned as Samuel grew older; they wanted someone they could rely upon, and they didn't trust Samuel's sons to carry on his work. His sons were blinded by power and the promise of riches and were unsuitable to succeed Samuel. (Read 1 Sam. 8:4–5.)

This was a defining moment in Israel's history. Despite Samuel's warnings about the potential dangers of having a ruler, the people persisted. God complied with the request but seemed to harbor misgivings and regrets about the decision.

There is great tension at this point in the story—tension among the tribes over who would be ruler; tension between Israel and the Philistines as they vied for the same land; and tension between the people and God as they sought to live into a new way of being.

THE LEADERSHIP THING: WHAT'S IT ALL ABOUT?

We will have opportunities to look at personality and leadership styles, in addition to the exciting stories of failures and victories of Israel's leaders. The merit of a ruler's leadership hinged on the ability to stay in line with God's will for Israel. As long as the ruler was faithful and obedient to God, God would bless the nation. The foibles of the ruler would have detrimental effects on the nation.

Ask a hundred people a simple question, "What is leadership?" and you are likely to get 150 different answers! "Leadership" is one of those words that everyone knows but no one can define. We are likely to tick off a list of qualities, positive and negative, rather than give a definitive answer to the question. The context within which the question is asked also shapes the answer. For example, is corporate business leadership different from religious leadership? Is leadership for a nonprofit social agency different than leadership for a Sunday school class? Is leadership for a youth group different than leadership for a nation? Is leadership the same as, different from, or complementary to management? Is there a difference between power and authority? Is leadership self-claimed or must others confer it? Is leadership the same as maintaining the status quo or does it include some sense of vision? Does character matter in leadership? If so, in what ways does character matter? How do we measure leadership effectiveness? Does personality play a role in leadership? This brief list of questions is only the tip of the leadership iceberg. And for our study, we must place God in the midst of leadership questions, issues, challenges, and concerns.

In the Bible, God has a lot to say about leadership. As ultimate authority in Israel, God picked and disposed of leaders for Israel. God's choices often defied all logic—it is difficult, almost impossible, to discern the criteria by which God chose leaders. We are dumbfounded at God's choices—it's easier to just declare that God's ways are a mystery!

- God called Moses to liberate the Hebrews from slavery, yet Moses was the privileged adopted grandson of Pharaoh and a murderous fugitive. God called Moses to articulate a vision of liberation and community, yet Moses was reluctant to act and had a serious speech impediment. God called Moses to lead the people through the wilderness to a promised land, yet Moses couldn't read a map, wouldn't ask for directions, was administratively challenged, and had anger management issues!

▪ God called Abraham to be the parent of a great nation, yet Abraham was an old man married to a barren woman who was already way past her childbearing prime. God called Abraham to develop a strong nation, yet Abraham allowed his wife to abuse his baby Ishmael's mother Hagar, and he banished Hagar and son from his home, not once, but twice! God called Abraham to exemplify character, yet Abraham lied and cheated to save his own skin and came only inches away from slaughtering his second son, Isaac.

▪ God called Jacob to establish God's name in the promised land, yet Jacob tricked his older brother out of his birthright and, in cahoots with his mother, deceived his father into blessing him over Esau. Jacob was slow to learn the ways of God. Jacob was forced into the wilderness to fend for himself, was lied to and deceived by his own uncle, and battled with an angel to the verge of death before he got it—that to be a leader requires much more than blind ambition!

Then, there's the unstable business of the judges. God waited until there was a crisis before raising up and empowering a leader to deal with particular problems. At first, God chose able, competent leaders to handle military and other situations: Deborah and Gideon are all right; but Jephthah and Samson are messes. Samuel proved to be a pretty good leader, and he wanted his sons to carry on his work. But they were evil scoundrels; no way would the elders follow them. And so we come to the moment when the elders stated clearly that God has fallen down on the job and they wanted a ruler. The burning question was, what would a ruler do for Israel that

Samuel and YHWH had not? This brings us back to the question, "What is leadership?"

Leadership, simply stated, is the ability or capacity to get things done using a variety of resources. This general definition provides the stage to talk about a number of issues. My assumption about leadership is twofold.

The first assumption is that who I am matters! I am influenced by factors such as gender, age, class, race, sexuality, religious background, and social and cultural background. Any of these factors might bring with them discrimination and oppression. How I react to that discrimination determines how I see the world. If I see myself as a victim, I might react in hostility. If I see myself as the captain of my fate and undeterred by obstacles, I might react boldly and innovatively as I challenge the status quo. My background may empower me or weigh me down in guilt and insecurity. Or my background may give me a sense of privilege and entitlement that oppresses and offends others. I may move in the world with dignity, serenity, and courage or with arrogance and insensitivity. I may be fully present in situations or I may seek to escape them. I may seek acceptance and approval or I may be distant and aloof. I may embrace life or rebel against it. I may be joyful or pitiful. I may participate in life with joy and humility or with sarcasm and anger. In other words, my social location and theological understandings shape how I see the world, how I understand my choices, and how I make decisions and understand outcomes of my decisions. Some self-understanding enables me to balance my dreams and needs and my contribution to community as well helps me clarify my values and determine what is really important. All of this matters when we look at leadership styles and effectiveness. It is important to have a realistic sense of our strengths and weaknesses and to be open to constructive criticism from others.

The second assumption is that what I do matters! How I behave as a leader is determined by who I am and I cannot separate who I am from what I do. All of my choices are rooted in my understanding of who I am (or am perceived to be)—I don't make decisions in a vacuum. I bring all of myself to every decision and choice. Still, I must be able to bring something of substance to the leadership enterprise. Leaders face ethical dilemmas, and how they deal with those dilemmas determines their effectiveness. Leaders must have certain skills—administrative and people skills—in order to set forth a vision and implement it. Leaders must understand their context and recognize those things that will help or hinder progress. In addition, leaders need problem-solving skills. Leaders should be risk-takers and understand consequences. All of these are important for effective leadership—leaders get things done.

Most leaders have to deal with two important issues: change and conflict. It has been said that the only constant in life is change. However, many of us resist change; we behave as if denial will stop things from changing. But nothing could be further from the truth—change happens, whether we embrace it or shun it. Change makes us feel overwhelmed and frustrated and confused. Instead of seeing change as an opportunity for innovation, flexibility, and clarification, we resent change and see it as an obstacle to be overcome. Change can be a constructive push to deeper wisdom, maturity, and effectiveness.

As we will see in the Bible studies to follow, what is at stake is finding a way to balance the old with the new. Those stuck in the old ways fail to recognize the adventure that lies ahead. Those bent on doing a new thing fail to recognize the wisdom and legacy of the old. When we are able to see change as an opportunity, we are open to new possibilities; we see resources previously hidden and directions that will make a difference.

Samuel is an example of one who does not deal well with change. Samuel was definitely "old school." For him, the old ways were just fine and there was no need to change anything. But as Israel's circumstances changed and evolved, there was a need for a different kind of leadership. His passive-aggressive stand on rulership created headaches for Saul that continued into David's reign.

Change should invite us to reflect on and evaluate our situation and circumstance. Change should invite us to brainstorm solutions to problems and discover new ways of doing things. Change should foster confidence as we test strategies and get input from others. Most of the time, however, change divides us and undermines a sense of teamwork and community. Change becomes a struggle between those who want to cling to the past and those who want to forge into the future. Change has the potential to build community and to share leadership. Change can be a great adventure if we keep open minds and are willing to take some risks. In the midst of change, we have a chance to determine what is really important and what can be cast aside or reworked to fit new circumstances and situations.

Wherever two or three are gathered, there is bound to be conflict sooner or later. Conflict can be a simple disagreement or all-out war. We are used to seeing conflict as a negative thing that tears families, communities, and organizations apart. We see conflict as something that is disruptive and painful and leaves people feeling like victims. Conflict can lead to disillusionment, apathy, alienation, isolation, and distrust. Conflictual situations can open the way for persons to be abused, neglected, and harassed. On the other hand, conflict can serve a positive function—leading to innovation and new or renewed interest. Conflict can bring out the strengths of persons and organizations.

Too often, conflict makes people act in strange ways. People can behave in autocratic, dictatorial, and stubborn ways. Sometimes, those in charge fail to deal with conflict, which leads to even more conflict. The thing to remember is that conflict doesn't just go away—it must be dealt with so that balance and harmony are restored. The aim of conflict management or conflict resolution is a win-win situation and some sense of reconciliation. Both parties must feel heard and taken seriously.

At the very least, conflict should give pause to revisit the vision, beliefs, mission, and values of the community or organization. There are a number of causes of conflict:

- Personality: conflicts occur when persons bring their individual agendas or needs to a given situation. Some folk want to fit in, some want to be in charge, some want to be the star. When they don't get what they want, they find ways to undermine the organization—they "act out" and cause problems. When people fail to have their needs met, they may become complainers, whiners, backstabbers, gossips, apathetic, or mean. Personality conflicts require someone who knows and understands human nature and is willing to confront a problem person.

- The organization itself: conflicts occur when persons don't understand the mission of the organization or when the organization tries to be too many things to too many people. The organization competes against itself with no clear vision or mission. People have a difficult time figuring out where they fit in and what they are supposed to do and why what they do is important. These kinds of conflict require someone who can clarify the vision and mission of the organization.

- Lack of clarity about roles: conflicts occur when people don't understand a chain of command that is logical and fair. Too many people vying for leadership positions with no clear understanding of what needs to happen to make the organization efficient is a common problem. Those in power positions need to be given enough authority to carry out their jobs. Such conflicts require clear policies that are widely communicated.

- Lack of adequate organizational structure: conflicts occur when it is not clear who makes decisions or how decisions are made. Conflict issues arise when there are no established policies or inadequate ones. Such conflicts require clear guidelines for decision-making processes. Functions and tasks need to be clearly outlined and communicated. Lines of accountability also need to be clear. The more transparent the process, the less intense the conflict will be.

- Lack of adequate communication: most conflicts arise because there are failures to communicate. Even with our electronic, lightning fast communication, misunderstandings abound. In addition, there is often a failure to communicate with the right people. At issue is how information is conveyed—who is left out and who is ignored? Lack of communication leads to gossip and rumors that can greatly undermine the effectiveness of any organization. Certainly, families are torn apart because of communication failures, and the same is true for organizations. Such conflicts require the constant sharing of information, programs, goals, needs, and opportunities.

Conflict management is about negotiation and compromise. Good leaders are willing to deal with conflict head-on, are not afraid of confrontation, are willing to make tough decisions, understand power dynamics and human nature, deal with reality rather than with assumptions, keep the big picture in view, understand what is driving the conflict, are fair, can be trusted to be honest, and are detached enough to see the situation objectively. Every member of an organization needs to feel welcomed and valued. People need to know what will happen to them and what contribution they can make. People also want to have confidence in their leaders—to know that the leaders are fair, trustworthy, and loyal to the goals of the organization and to the people who support them. And always, each member needs to hear "thank you" on a regular basis. Conflict can be an opportunity for growth and learning as long as those in charge are willing to deal with situations in healthy ways.

Of course, no discussion about leadership is complete without exploring the issue of power. Most of us are ambivalent about power—we say we have none and often feel victimized by those who have power. What we are reacting to is a misuse or abuse of power. Power itself is neutral—it is simply the capacity or ability to get something done. If there is no power, there is no action. The task is to determine the difference between effective use of power rather than an abusive or exploitative use of power. We all have power, whether we realize it or claim it. How we use our power becomes the real issue. The use of power includes, or should include, some sense of ethics. That is, what motivates us to do what we do—do we have a vision of a common good or do we operate out of our own needs or insecurities?

While we each have personal power, there is also power that comes with one's status or position. And this raises the question about the difference between power and authority. For instance, the rulers in Israel had power and authority—granted by the people and ultimately granted by God. There are measures by which people give their consent for one to lead them. God gave the authority for the rulers to exercise their power—but there were limits on what God permitted and what God prohibited. When the rulers overstepped their bounds, they were punished and held accountable.

We will see that the rulers of Israel all wrestled with power and authority and dealt with change and conflict. They were constantly trying to balance their own self-interest and God's will for their work. Like them, we too must constantly reflect on how much of what we do in the church, the community, and the world stems from the rewards we expect and how much stems from a true perceived call from God—is it about me or is it about God? How can we tell? To whom are we accountable? What happens when our self-interests outweigh the good that God expects?

THE WAR THING: THE RULER AS WARRIOR

The stories found in Judges, 1 and 2 Samuel, and 1 and 2 Kings are among the bloodiest ones in the Bible and in literature. Our modern sensibilities are offended when we read that God not only sanctioned but also commanded the wholesale destruction of cities and human beings to be burned and killed. The notion of "holy war" does not play well in our culture. We have lived with wars and rumors of war and we are able to talk about war in political, economic, and social terms. But to talk about war in spiritual terms takes us into uncomfortable territory. Today, many of us are pacifists and feel that disputes are best settled diplomatically. We work for peace and protest war in the many forms it takes today. Such was not always the case in biblical times.

The D tradition highlights that the main goal of Israel was to remain pure and uncontaminated by its neighbors. Every attempt was made to keep Israel holy and faithful to the one God, YHWH. The shapers of the tradition felt that any and all means had to be used in order to keep Israel true to its mission—to show other nations what it was like to live under God's reign. They felt that purity was the order of the day. The people of Israel were to place their utmost devotion in the one true God and to rely on that God for all of their needs and desires. By keeping the laws of Moses, the people were guaranteed prosperity and longevity. The D tradition held these beliefs because of the miraculous way in which the Hebrews were freed from Egyptian oppression—what a mighty God had intervened on their behalf and brought them deliverance and liberation. Anything other than total reliance on God resulted in bad things. The impending doom that hung over Israel was twofold: that the nation would be separated from God forever and that the nation would be exiled from the land that God had promised. The people had fought so hard to occupy the land, but their success was a reflection of God's mercy and care for them. To lose the land would be an affront to the God who worked so diligently to free them from slavery and establish a community that recognized God's sovereignty and power. So if war was required to keep Israel pure, then war it would be. (Read Deut. 20:10–18.)

War itself was not praised in the Hebrew Bible; victories were seen as the work of God and it was God who was praised. Israel's work was to settle into the land God had promised to them. They could not do so without going to war with the nations already occupying the land. Efforts at diplomacy were often frustrating and treaties were often broken. There were always "new kids on the block" who tried to flex their muscles against Israel, and the nation had to defend itself. So we have numerous stories about war that reflect Israel's attempt to settle in the land.

Not surprisingly, one important image of God for Israel is that of "warrior ruler." Israel would not exist if God had not gone to war with Egypt to liberate the Hebrew slaves from oppression. In delivering and liberating the slaves, God seemed to set the stage for ongoing war. (Read Exod. 15:3–4 and Josh. 1:2–7.)

Israel understood that God was on their side and intervened in its history to keep the nation strong and safe. Israel's enemies were also God's enemies. God helped Israel when the nation went to war. God provided strength, courage, and even military strategies. In fact, God fought Israel's battles and no war was won without the explicit help of God. (Read Exod. 14:13–14 and 1 Sam. 14:23.)

The primary word in Hebrew for war is *milchamah*; its root *lacham* carries a wide range of meaning, from consuming, devouring, overcoming, crowding, and jostling to armed conflict and antagonism. There are over three hundred references to war in the Hebrew Bible. War is the result of conflict between two or more groups of people. Wars are fought for political, economic, social, and religious reasons. While war is prominent in the Hebrew Bible, there is no specific reference to "holy war." However, it is clear that God sanctioned and even commanded the nation to fight wars and battles. One did not dare go to war without first asking if God wanted it; in this way, God gave victory. (Read Josh. 8:1–2 and 2 Kgs 3:18–19.)

God was a living, active force in the life of Israel. God not only used war to the advantage of Israel, but also used war to teach the people lessons. And Israel was "punished" through the means of war. Whenever Israel failed to win a war, it was because God had withdrawn divine power from the nation. That is, as long as Israel was faithful and obedient to God, the nation fared well. War language was used to highlight God's judgment for or against Israel. When the nation turned away from God, it experienced defeat and oppression. (Read Jer. 5:15–19.)

In Israel's history, we find the nation spending a lot of time, effort, and money either preparing for war or actually engaging in war.

In this way, Israel was just like its neighbors. Israel's mission was to settle into the land that God promised; to Israel's surprise, there were already people occupying the land. During this period, many peoples were migrating and settling in new lands. The reasons were varied: to escape famine, to find suitable grazing land for cattle and suitable land for farming, to find new sources of fresh water, to claim new territory for expansion, or to escape oppression. The ancient world was on the move and Israel was no exception.

It was inevitable that there would be conflicts over territory and Israel's early history is about war and violence. Israel did not differ from its neighbors—all were vying for space to live. In fact, Israel's monarchy was established and maintained by engaging in war; we know so many people in the Bible because of their military exploits. Joshua, Deborah, Gideon, Saul, and David are big personalities because they went to war and won.

The tribes faced a major threat in the Philistines, and the old ways of rallying the tribes was not working. Samuel's national leadership was based in his ability to head up Israel's military efforts. However, Israel was totally intimidated by the Philistines, who were bigger, stronger, more heavily armed, and more organized. Israel needed a ruler to help them fight. In fact, their request for a ruler revolved around the whole war thing. (Read 1 Sam. 8:19–20.)

During the monarchy, Israel seems to have been constantly engaged in war. The northern tribes and southern tribes not only fought each other, they also fought other nations. The tribes sometimes formed alliances to fight a common enemy and they also fought on their own. It took a while to subdue the Philistines, and at the same time there were campaigns by other nations: the Amalekites, Arameans, Syrians, Moabites, Amorites, Hizzites, Ammonites, Midianites, and a host of others.

Despite the continual presence of and engagement in war, the ideal state for Israel was not war but rather *shalom* (peace)—not just the absence of war, but the well-being of all people. The word implies a wholeness that includes personal and communal well-being. *Shalom* covers a wide range of concerns: plentiful harvests, rest from war and fighting, safety from wild animals, health, contentment, and the presence of joy and righteousness. (Read Lev. 26:6–11 and Ps. 120:7.)

Israel's existence and well-being depended on God's mercy and justice. Peace was a gift from God to a people who were faithful.

> *Let me hear what God [YHWH] will speak,*
> *for [God] will speak peace to[God's] people,*
> *to [God's] faithful, to those who turn to [God] in*
> *their hearts. (Ps. 85:8)*

The pictures of God that emerge from these stories leave us uneasy. However, the tradition was trying to convey the seriousness of Israel's mission—to exemplify justice and compassion in community. Thus, Israel was challenged by the prophets to care for widows and orphans, to show hospitality to the stranger, to treat each other fairly, to be compassionate to others as God had been compassionate to them, to treat all creation with kindness, to take only what they needed and not lapse into mindless consumerism and exploitation, to settle disputes with diplomacy—if Israel followed these guidelines for communal life, all would go well. If Israel did not, then the nation could expect to deal with consequences and repercussions. These stories in the books of Samuel, Kings, and Chronicles are snapshots of Israel's attempt to live holy and wholly to God.

We will find mirrored in these stories our own concerns about justice, community, the viability and purposes of political processes, and the tension between self-interest and the common good. We will reflect on leadership concerns such as vision, values, integrity, accountability, power and authority, conflict management and resolution, relationships, and change. These stories have implications for how we behave and how we exercise leadership both in the church and in the society at large.

Now, it is time to take a closer look at what happens when the people ask for and receive their ruler—like the other nations!

1 · SAMUEL

WHY CAN'T I BE THE MAN?

Read 1 Samuel 2:1–10, 12:1–25

Samuel, great prophet of God, brought a great deal of drama to the biblical story. His story began with the prayers of his mother and resulted in his work as one who anointed, counseled, and dismissed rulers. Samuel had his own issues with rulership and it is not easy to determine whether his feelings were rooted in his spirituality or his ego.

The issue of rulership for Israel revolved around a simple question: Who is the man? Israel's history of the monarchy hinged on the answer to this question. And, unfortunately, the answers too often proved wrong. As we watch Israel move into the monarchy, we see how inept they were—they had only the examples of the surrounding nations as models. And certainly, they wished not to repeat the horrors they had experienced under Egyptian monarchy. With no effective role models, Israel stumbled through the early days of the monarchy and their efforts left much to be desired.

No study of the monarchy can begin without a look at Hannah. In fact, in very real ways, the monarchy begins with Hannah—her pain, her struggle, her prayers, and finally her celebration of God's grace when she dedicated her son to God are symbolic of God's dealings with the nation. Hannah was verbal and political. She talked about the joy of children and political structures. She had something to say to the haves on behalf of the have-nots—while she rejoiced in her own personal joy, she also lifted up national concerns for others who were on the edges of society. The bottom line for Hannah and for Israel was gratefulness to God for God's gifts of life.

Hannah was married to Elkanah, a well-to-do leader in his hometown. It was in the best interest of women to marry men who were able to take care of them and provide a good life. The role of wife was tied to that of motherhood. Therefore, the "barren" wife was cause for concern in the Bible. Her infertility threatened the very future of the family and left her vulnerable to abandonment and poverty. Barrenness threatened God's ability to deliver what God promised. The statement that a woman was barren heightened the tension in the narrative. Every means available was to be used to ensure heirs, especially male heirs, for the husband. It was believed that infertility was the work of God, who closed up the wombs of women for various reasons.

The barren woman was not a new phenomenon in Israel—Sarah was barren; Rachel was barren—and it was believed that barren women were cursed. If barren women later gave birth to sons, it was considered a miracle and gift from God. In many cases, the son was specially anointed to further God's work in the world.

Isaac and Jacob, both born to previously barren women, were major players in God's efforts to bring something new to creation and the world. And so we anticipate something special when we learn that Hannah was unable to have children. But Elkanah had another wife, Peninnah. Peninnah was quite fertile and provided sons and daughters for her husband. In the pattern portrayed in Genesis between Sarah and Hagar, Peninnah flaunted her fertility and made Hannah feel inferior. In fact, she provoked Hannah and made her life miserable.

Each year, Elkanah and his family made a pilgrimage to Shiloh to leave their offerings to God and to seek God's blessings and grace. In addition, he offered gifts to his wives and for his children. Peninnah received a share according to the number of children she had borne; Hannah received a double portion even though she did not deserve it because she had no children. Her husband loved her and did not want her to feel left out or neglected. But Peninnah tormented Hannah and nothing could console her. In fact, Peninnah practically tortured Hannah to the point where she was sad and refused to eat (see 1 Sam. 1:6–7).

Elkanah obviously loved Hannah and asked about her state of mind. In an attempt to express his love for her, he actually admonished her and made her pain greater: "Am I not more to you than ten sons?" (1 Sam. 1:8b). His question does not show much understanding of Hannah's plight. Hannah's life would be fine and set as long as her husband lived. But if something should happen, if he died before she did, she would have to rely on the kindness of strangers with no guarantee that she would have what she needed to survive. With no sons to take her in and provide for her, Hannah would be a troublesome widow whom others would grow to resent and ostracize. So her weeping and wailing at Shiloh was not about whether her husband loved her, but rather about what would happen to her when her husband died. Her weeping and wailing was not about whether her husband provided a good life now but rather whether she would have a life after he was gone. Her weeping and wailing was not about the present comfort her husband provided but rather about whether the future would hold comfort or homelessness and hunger.

Hannah fervently prayed to God for a child, a son. And if God granted her petition, Hannah promised to dedicate her son to the service of God—she was willing to give her son as a gift back to God. He would be dedicated to God's service as a Nazirite, just as Samson was. (Read 1 Sam. 1:11.)

The priest Eli, the keeper of the sacred place, misunderstood her actions and assumed that she was drunk! Now, how he reached that conclusion is puzzling. It is not clear whether he was surprised to see a woman in prayer or that he had not seen anyone totally caught up in his or her prayer. Even when Hannah corrected his assumption, he did not offer any pastoral care for her. He did not ask what she was praying for and did not offer to pray with her. She told him she was deeply troubled and was pouring her heart out to God. It is clear that she really wanted someone to understand her situation and to offer help. She revealed that her prayers come from her anxiety and worry. She gave him two chances to help, but Eli dismissed her as if he didn't hear the desperation in her voice. Either he did not understand or he did not care about her and her situation. He merely sent her on her way (see 1 Sam. 1:12–18).

Shortly after their pilgrimage to Shiloh, Hannah became pregnant and gave birth to Samuel. In due time, Elkanah and she took Samuel to Shiloh, where he was given to the same priest, Eli, who had dismissed Hannah. She reminded him of who she was and left her son in Eli's care. She celebrated by reciting a prayer, which is commonly known as the Song of Hannah. Scholars believe that her song echoes an ancient public hymn of Israel. The song speaks of national and public matters and emphasizes God's awesome and life-giving power. The song serves a double purpose: to praise God for Samuel and to point to matters of rulership, especially the reign of David. In this way, Israel tied together the personal and public dimensions of its life.

Hannah praised God for the precious gift of her son—God had opened her womb and blessed her beyond belief. Her song, though, took on a communal tone. In fact, her song seemed to be a warning about God and rulers! In a real sense the story of the monarchy began not with Saul but with Hannah. Hannah's song is a vision of what life will be like under the leadership of rulers.

Hannah was a pitiful woman who was waiting for something that might not happen. Hannah was childless and had no logical reason to think that she would have a baby. She placed her hope in God and prayed for what she desired. She hoped that God would remember her and grant her wish.

Hannah symbolizes the hapless nation Israel—the nation was overwhelmed and intimidated by its enemies. Because of Israel's size and style of life (living under the reign of God), it had no logical reason to think that it would actually dominate the land God had promised. Israel hoped that God would remember the nation and would send them what they needed. Hannah prayed to God for a miracle; Israel sought a ruler.

Both Hannah and Israel were waiting, hoping, and watching to see what God would do. Waiting is a hard thing to do—we have little patience with waiting. We want things to happen instantly and to our specifications. Hannah prayed and felt better, knowing she had left her concerns, worries, and anxieties with God. She could only hope that God heard her prayer. She knew that if anyone could help her, it was God. After pouring her heart out to God, she felt better and was able to eat and move on with her life. While there was no logical reason to hope for a miracle, she hoped anyway. When Hannah became pregnant, she realized that her miracle was not merely a matter of biology—God had heard her prayer and remembered her. Samuel was born and given back to God in gratitude. The song highlights issues regarding God's power and a series of reversals: the mighty are brought down while the helpless are exalted; the full are hungry while the hungry are fed; the barren one brings life while the fertile lose life; the rich become poor while the poor are raised up. And Hannah set forth a job description for the coming ruler: he would work on behalf of the poor, the needy, the hungry, and the barren. In other words, the ruler was not in office for power and control but rather to serve and to protect.

In the meantime, Samuel was raised and mentored by Eli, who was faithful to God. Eli taught Samuel what he knew, knowledge that was firmly rooted in the teachings of Moses. Eli recognized that God had called Samuel for a special purpose. Eli acknowledged that his own sons were not worthy of leadership—they were described as scoundrels.

Israel was facing annihilation at the hands of the Philistines. If something didn't happen soon, Israel would be conquered and possibly wiped out. Things didn't look good for Israel; the book of Judges ends with the statement that "the people did what is good in their own eyes" because there was no ruler (Judg. 21:25). At Shiloh, we find old Eli, who had remained faithful to God and his priestly duties. But Eli's sons were a mess and the people refused to follow them or even claim them as leaders. So here the nation was—without adequate leadership and trying to survive. But Samuel was the man who saved Israel.

Samuel was anointed and authorized to work on Israel's behalf—he was priest, warrior, and prophet. (Read 1 Sam. 3:19–4:1.)

Samuel was a national leader and the people looked up to him. Samuel was competent, fair, and dependable. He enjoyed an ongoing intimate relationship with God. Samuel mediated between the people and God—encouraging the people to maintain their covenant agreements so that God would continue blessing them. This was clearly "old school" theology that had ties to Mosaic teachings (see 1 Sam. 7:3-4). Samuel's role was similar to that of Moses—admonishing Israel to embrace no other gods, only YHWH. The challenge was to remain true to YHWH in the midst of the Philistine threat, Canaanite culture, and Canaanite religion. Israel was tempted to embrace the ways of the people who surrounded them. No doubt there were things about their neighbors that were attractive to Israel, and holding to its foundation must have been challenging. Yet Samuel reminded the people that their life, security, and well-being depended on their sole reliance on YHWH.

Samuel provided good leadership for Israel. He appointed his sons as leaders over Israel. His sons, Joel and Abijah, however, failed to live up to their father's high standards. They took bribes and perverted justice (see 1 Sam. 8:3). And this is when the trouble started. Unlike Eli, Samuel did nothing to call his sons to task. He let them do whatever they wanted even though he knew better. The people were not about to let Samuel's evil sons lead them—they asked for a ruler. The grand experiment with judges and prophets and priests would not work if the leaders didn't follow the ways of God.

All the elders approached Samuel with their request. Some scholars question the motives of the elders—the elders would stand to benefit from having a ruler. A ruler would maintain their economic and social status. Their initial request reflected their concern that Samuel was old and his sons were wayward:

> *You are old and your sons do not follow in your ways;*
> *appoint for us, then, a ruler to govern us, like other nations.*
> (1 Sam. 8:5)

Samuel's reaction to their request is curious—he was displeased. Now, why would he have a reaction to their request? We must remember that since the days of Eli, Samuel had been "the man." He had been in charge of the nation; he traveled a circuit to mediate conflicts, to settle disputes, and to administer the sacraments and rituals central to Israel's worship life. Samuel had single-handedly held the nation together with the help of God. It is safe to suggest that Samuel had enjoyed all the perks that come with being in charge—the respect, the admiration, and the power. Samuel alone had shouldered the burden of overseeing the well-being of the nation, he alone had mapped out military strategies, he alone had prayed to God on behalf of the people. And now that Samuel was old and near retirement, he wanted his sons to carry on his work and legacy. But the people did not want to see Samuel's line continue in leadership. His sons violated the basic tenets of Mosaic faith by not practicing justice for all members of the community. The request for a ruler struck at the heart of what made Israel different from the other nations; now they wanted to be just like the very things that God had said they should not.

I imagine that Samuel was angry—after all he had done, this was the thanks he got. He was so angry and hurt that he prayed to God. God recognized that Samuel was not thinking clearly—Samuel thought the matter was about him, but God assured him that he had provided good leadership. At stake was the realization that the elders didn't want to live under God's leadership anymore, and they told Samuel as much. (Read 1 Sam. 8:7–9.)

It seems that both Samuel and God were upset. Both felt rejected. Why didn't God just refuse or ignore the elders' request? Instead, God acquiesced to their demand, but we have the sense that God was not happy about it. It is interesting that Samuel did not tell the elders that God would grant them a ruler; instead, he launched into warnings. He told them what they could expect from a ruler, and none of it was flattering. A ruler would violate the public trust and abuse power and authority:

- A ruler would draft their sons to fight wars and build weapons.
- A ruler would enlist their daughters to serve the court.
- A ruler would take their fields, vineyards, and orchards in taxes.
- A ruler would take a tithe of production for the state.
- A ruler would make sure the ruler's buddies were taken care of at the expense of the people.
- A ruler would alienate the people from God, who would then withdraw support in the time of need.

Samuel really tried to put a scare into the people by stating that a ruler would enslave them—they would be back where they were under Egyptian rule. But Samuel's warning fell on deaf ears; the people were desperate for security and stuck with their request. (Read 1 Sam. 8:19–22.)

The people, and not just the elders, grew emphatic that they wanted a ruler. This time, they laid out their vision: to be like the other nations, to have a permanent leader, and to have a leader to fight their battles. It is interesting to note the resignation in God's response to

Samuel, and even more interesting that Samuel did not tell the people that God has consented to appoint a ruler over them. This is only the first of several times when Samuel did not deliver the whole message. It is interesting to wonder why Samuel withheld important information. The issue would come up again in his dealings with Saul.

Samuel followed God's orders and appointed Saul to be the first ruler of Israel. Samuel served as Saul's prophet—a role that included advice and mediation between the ruler and God. Samuel seemed to resent his new job description. He had gone from *being* the man to *serving* the man—what a shift for him. Samuel may have been suffering, too, from burnout. He was older and perhaps a bit slower than when he first assumed his work as a national leader.

At any rate, we question Samuel's sincerity in his work with Saul. Samuel withheld information and undermined Saul's leadership. In one instance, he advised Saul to wait for seven days before going into battle. Samuel promised to show up on the seventh day to advise Saul. But for unknown reasons, Samuel did not arrive at the appointed time. Saul had no choice but to act; and under normal circumstances, the initiative of the ruler would be rewarded. Instead, Samuel used the occasion to fire Saul. He dismissed Saul's attempt to explain and walked away. On another occasion, Samuel chastised Saul for not finishing a job that God had given him. Samuel showed up and finished the job with much anger—he humiliated Saul and saw nothing wrong with his actions.

Samuel reached the end of his rope and decided to retire from active duty. In most cases, when a person retires, adoring coworkers and colleagues fete him or her. But Samuel threw his own retirement party. And instead of celebrating his accomplishments and wishing the people well, he used the occasion to blast the people and to question their loyalty to him.

In 1 Samuel 12:1–25, Samuel made it clear that the people got what they wanted and what a pitiful choice it was. He challenged the people to find anything wrong with his leadership. He asked if he ever took what didn't belong to him, if he ever cheated anyone, if he ever accepted a bribe, if he ever unfairly judged a case—he dared them to state one instance when he hadn't fulfilled his duty. Of course, the people could not cite an instance, for Samuel had ruled well. But the people were probably shocked to be put on the defensive. Some probably wondered if Samuel had lost his mind—where was he coming from with these serious questions, seemingly out of the blue? Samuel even used God as a witness to his fitness for leadership.

I imagine the people muttered among themselves about Samuel's actions and questions. And he didn't let up—he kept right on with his tirade but never once mentions his evil sons. He recited the history of the people with God—God's intervention to bring their liberation, God's care during the wilderness wanderings, God's protection as they claimed the promised land—and after all that God (and Samuel) had done for them, they still insisted on a ruler. So they got what they asked for and deserved. He again issued the warning that if the ruler followed in the ways of God, all would be well. But if the ruler failed in any way, the people would suffer for sure. Then, Samuel performed a mighty act of calling down rain during the wheat harvest, a customary dry season.

The people tried to reassure Samuel that they had no problems with his leadership. Their request for a ruler was not an indictment on him. They liked Samuel and appreciated all that he had done for Israel, but it was time for new leadership. They did not trust his sons to carry on the work that was so crucial to their life. Of course, the request for a ruler implied that the people could do for themselves what God had been doing since their liberation from Egypt. They subtly said they could do a better job than God. Still they recognized that they were God's people and could not totally govern themselves. They begged Samuel to not be angry with them and to continue praying for them. Samuel begrudgingly agreed, not because it was his joy but rather to keep God from jumping on him:

> *Moreover as for me, far be it from me that I should sin against [YHWH] by ceasing to pray for you; and I will instruct you in the good and the right way.* (1 Sam. 12:23)

At this point, Saul took center stage. Samuel worked behind the scene to hold Saul accountable to God and to the people. But Samuel seemed to take joy in undermining Saul's work and used any opportunity to make Saul look foolish. It is as though Samuel pointed up Saul's shortcomings as a way of letting the people know the error of their ways in asking for a ruler.

It's not clear whether Samuel wanted to be ruler. On the one hand, he behaved in passive-aggressive ways to humiliate Saul. He seemed to take special joy in firing Saul from his position of ruler (see 1 Sam. 15).

Saul was instructed to attack the Amalekites. (Read 1 Sam. 15:1–3.) This is a passage that causes difficulty for modern sensibilities. Remember, though, that the D tradition is about religious purity and the command was directed to destroy any threat to that purity. The term "utterly destroy" (*herem* in Hebrew) means to put under the ban or destroy as a religious sacrifice (see Deut. 20:16–18). The language serves to underline what set Israel apart from other nations. Saul, however, did not carry out the *herem* and seemed to exercise his own judgment with compassion. Samuel implied that Saul couldn't even follow explicit orders; instead he tried to think and ended up messing up the whole operation. Samuel seemed resentful that Saul had the authority to act but couldn't even get his mission straight. And if it were not for Samuel, who knew what would have happened to the people?

On the other hand, we learn that Samuel grieved over Saul— but it is not clear what the basis of his grief was. We learn that God regretted the choice of Saul and perhaps Samuel agreed with God's assessment. Because of Saul, the people were on the verge of losing everything. But God stepped in and fussed at Samuel. (Read 1 Sam. 16:1–3.)

This was the beginning of the end for Saul and attention shifts from him to David—God's grand experiment to get the ruler-thing right. Samuel played a major role in the selection of a new ruler.

Samuel was not done with Saul yet, though; or rather, Saul was not done with Samuel. They had one last encounter late in Saul's reign. The Philistine reign of terror had intensified and Saul didn't know what to do. Saul had expended a lot of time, energy, and resources trying to get rid of David but now the Philistines were back on center stage. This time, the Philistines seemed bigger and stronger than ever and Saul was terrified. But as ruler, he had to fight. Saul prayed to God but God did not answer. Saul cast lots to inquire of God, but God was still silent. (Saul didn't realize that God had completely withdrawn from him and anointed David as the next ruler.)

In total desperation, Saul asked a seer to bring up Samuel's ghost (Samuel had died some time before). She called up Samuel's ghost, who did not like having his eternal bliss interrupted. He lashed out at Saul; their interaction is painful to read (1 Sam. 18:15–19). Saul poured out his heart to Samuel—he was in great distress over the Philistines, he felt abandoned because God wouldn't communicate with him, the prophets were ignoring him, and he was seeking Samuel for help. Samuel was downright mean to Saul and showed him no compassion or care—the scene is similar to that between Hannah and Eli. Samuel declared that he was done with Saul just as God was done with him. Not only that, God was Saul's enemy and now liked David. In fact, God was giving the territory to David and there was nothing Saul could do to stop it. Not only that, but on the very next day, Saul and his sons would die. Furthermore, the Philistines would prevail against Israel. Saul came to Samuel under the cloak of secrecy to seek his help. Samuel summarily dismissed him in brutal fashion.

So what can we say about Samuel and his leadership? Samuel was stuck in the middle between all that Israel had known and this new thing it was trying out. Samuel represented the interests of the old-timers. Samuel was not comfortable with the direction the nation was taking, but he couldn't just abandon his work. Samuel's boss was God and he took his orders from God. Despite Samuel's personal feelings, he still had to do what God told him. It is not clear if Samuel disliked Saul personally or if he harbored professional resentment against him. To his credit, Samuel was the founder of the prophetic movement in Israel. A primary responsibility of the prophet was to keep the ruler on track and in God's will. Samuel definitely kept Saul in check.

We suspect that Samuel relished his position of power and authority—he refused to go down without a fight. Samuel had been God's guy since the last of the judges. He stood in sharp contrast to previous judges—he was competent, obedient, and willing to serve. Israel's movement into the monarchy was a major shift and Samuel stood in the gap of the transition. The transition was political, economic, social, and religious—a drastic change. And Samuel had the task of managing change, training his successor, and remaining true to God's vision for the nation. Further, Samuel had to negotiate the transition; here he fell down on the communication front. He withheld information but held people accountable for that which they did not know. We can excuse some of this because Samuel did not have any role models for his transitional work. But he seemed intentionally to undermine and undercut Saul's leadership.

Samuel was a team player, but the team consists of God and him—Saul was left out of the loop. When Samuel interacted with Saul, it was under contentious circumstances. It was as though Saul couldn't do anything right and Samuel took glee in pointing out his shortcomings. We can't tell if Samuel was jealous or envious of Saul. We know that Samuel lacked pastoral care skills, both with the people and with Saul. Samuel came off as stern, cantankerous, rigid, and uncompromising. He lashed out for no good reason and never apologized for his demeanor. He didn't seem to care about anyone other than himself. He was a failure as a parent because he never held his sons accountable for their wicked ways; in fact, he never even acknowledged their shortcomings but made a big deal out of Saul's.

It could not have been easy for Samuel to watch the old ways pass away. The new way of the ruler just didn't feel right for him. But there was nothing he could do to stop the changes taking place in Israel. He had no choice but to give in to the people's wish for a ruler—the pressure is too great to resist. But Samuel was passive-aggressive with change and created problems for those trying to move forward. To his credit, he maintained an intimate relationship with God. But his relationships with his peers hinged on his being in power—he and Saul could have made a dynamic team, but he was not willing to share leadership with the new ruler. Samuel fired Saul and hired David, but played no significant role in David's reign.

We have to question God's role in Samuel's leadership adventure. If God had wholeheartedly supported Saul, perhaps Samuel would have made a better effort to work with him. But as it is, Samuel was at odds with Saul from the very beginning. There was nothing Saul could do to redeem himself in Samuel's eyes. The story played out and made Samuel look as bad as Saul. Samuel succumbed to social pressure from the people and was coerced by God into anointing not one, but two rulers.

Samuel, the miracle child born to a barren woman, was blessed with strong leadership skills. Those skills were developed under the able mentoring of Eli. Samuel was a strong leader, and people loved and respected him. But he was unapproachable; his anger resulted in humiliation for those who crossed him. We are left with a picture of Samuel that is complex—he was a good leader but not a nice person. He never got on board with the ruler-thing, and he left Saul high and dry. He never fully supported Saul and didn't try to hide his resentment and disgust. When he was no longer the man, Samuel retreated into animosity, sullenness, and hurt. His inability to overcome these feelings leaves a mar on his leadership record.

REFLECTION QUESTIONS

1. Do you think Samuel lived up to his mother's expectations of him?
2. Have you ever wanted a job that you didn't get? How did you handle the disappointment?
3. Who critiques or offers constructive feedback about your leadership? What do you learn from others?

4. How do you deal with change? Are your methods helping or hindering your leadership?

5. What makes you angry and/or resentful? How do you deal with these emotions?

6. Has your ego ever gotten in the way of sound or wise decisions? Explain.

7. Have you ever been jealous or envious of someone else? How did you handle the situation?

8. Why do you think Samuel ignored his sons' wickedness?

9. In what ways are you like Samuel? Explain.

10. If Samuel had his life to do over, what should he do differently?

2 · SAUL

I DON'T REALLY WANT TO BE THE MAN . . .

Read 1 Samuel 9:1–10:16, 13:7–15, 31:1–6

Saul was the first ruler of Israel, a job that had never been filled before. Saul stumbled through his reign—sometimes with competence and confidence and other times like a fool, inept and clueless. With no blueprint and only a scant job description, Saul improvised. Most scholars portray him as the tragic hero, as if he was responsible for his failure; in reality, his rulership was undermined from the very beginning by the prophet Samuel and by God.

Poor Saul! He was doomed before he even started. He had the thankless job of being Israel's first ruler—and he didn't want the job. When we first meet him, he is looking for his father's lost donkeys. Saul was the son of a wealthy man and had lived a life of privilege. Saul was a tall, handsome young man who seemed to have it all. He worked and seemed responsible if not a little unresourceful. His father, Kish, sent Saul and a servant to find some lost donkeys and bring them home. They searched high and low for the donkeys but could not find them. Saul wanted to go home so his father didn't worry about him and the other searchers. The servant, however, suggested they visit a man who might be able to help them; his remarks were telling. (Read 1 Sam. 9:6.)

The man they sought was none other than Samuel. And were they in for a surprise. At the start, Saul was reluctant to go to Samuel because they had no gift with which to pay or thank him. The servant offered his quarter shekel of silver, which Saul accepted. And off they went to see the "seer." The D storyteller inserted that, in those days, the seer was now known as a prophet. As they traveled up the hill to the city, they encountered a group of girls, who excitedly told them where to find Samuel. They finally approached Samuel, who had been told the day before to expect a visit from Israel's new ruler.

Samuel did not immediately tell Saul the groundbreaking news—that Saul was on a new journey as Israel's first ruler. Samuel withheld that vital information until the next day. At the break of dawn, Samuel anointed Saul with oil in a private ceremony and gave him his new job description. (Read 1 Sam. 10:1.)

Samuel went on to tell Saul what would happen as he continued his journey, including a meeting with a band of prophets. Saul would join in their prophetic frenzy as a sign that God had called him to be ruler. And Samuel's words came to pass:

> As [Saul] turned away to leave Samuel, God gave him
> another heart; and all these signs were fulfilled that day.
> (1 Sam. 10:9)

Saul made his way home, a different and changed man. His behavior with the prophets prompted the community to ask if it was really Saul! All that had happened to him probably overwhelmed Saul. He obviously needed time to process the events of the day; so when his uncle asked about his whereabouts, Saul gave him only partial information. There is no indication that Saul said anything about the events to his father. After such a momentous day, Saul didn't know what to do, so he just went home.

I'm sure Saul wished there had been a seminary or training program to help him grow into his role as ruler. It is clear that he had no idea what it meant to be ruler. He was forced to make up his job as he went along. He went back to his old life—living with and working for his father. What a way to start a new job.

At some point after anointing Saul, Samuel called a national meeting at Mizpah. There he launched again into his spiel about the peoples' request for a ruler (read 1 Sam. 10:17–19). Samuel cast lots to reveal to the people who God's choice for ruler was. The people were excited and impressed with Saul—after all, he was tall, handsome, and came from a good family. As the lot fell on Saul, he was nowhere to be found. Imagine that—the moment of the great revealing and Saul was hiding in the baggage! Now not only did Samuel question Saul as God's choice but so did the people—and with good cause. Who wants a ruler who hides from the job? Samuel's announcement carried a sarcastic note. (Read 1 Sam. 10:24.)

Samuel's comments can be viewed as a positive assessment or a negative one. He made his comments after Saul was pulled out from his hiding place—we would think that a ruler-elect would be proud, regal, ready to take office. But Saul was hiding; we don't know why he is in hiding—was he shy or just reluctant to assume leadership? Samuel seemed to be mocking the people, "See, this is what you wanted; and now you have it. Good luck—you deserve each other."

After giving the ruler and the people instructions about their new relationship, Samuel sent the people back home. With no palace to go to, Saul went home like everybody else. What a start to the monarchy—Saul went back to tend his father's donkeys. And the question raised by some "worthless" guys cuts to the quick:

> *But some worthless fellows said, "How can this man save us?" They despised [Saul] and brought him no present. But he held his peace. (1 Sam. 10:27)*

It is not clear who the "he" is in the last sentence. Neither Samuel nor Saul responds. But the question hovers over Saul's reign because we are not sure how Saul will save the people. His only role models were the rulers of the nations that harassed and oppressed his own nation. He had no mentors or examples to follow. Although Samuel had provided some guidelines, we will see that Saul really couldn't depend on Samuel to help him.

Saul's chance to be ruler soon emerged. We learn that Nahash, the ruler of the Ammonites, had been torturing the Gadites and Reubenites—he gouged out the right eyes of the men. Somehow, seven thousand men escaped to Jabesh-gilead; and a month later, Nahash invaded that city. After a diplomatic attempt failed, they asked for time to find someone to fight for them. Nahash, thinking his victory over the men of Jabesh-gilead was a done deal, granted the reprieve. This was no national emergency but did provide an opportunity for Saul to exercise leadership. And Saul did just that. When he heard what was happening to his kinfolk, Saul was struck by God's Spirit and sprung into action. (Read 1 Sam. 11:6–7.)

Saul took charge and led the people into battle. It is interesting to note that Saul called the men to battle, the job that Samuel used to do. But Saul included Samuel in his appeal to the others. Saul showed he was the right choice for ruler—he was courageous and exercised keen military acumen. After his show of bravery and competence, the people wanted to kill those who questioned Saul's right to be ruler. Rather than seek revenge, Saul shrugged off the insult and acknowledged that his success belongs to God:

> *But Saul said, "No one shall be put to death this day,*
> *for today [YHWH] has brought deliverance to Israel."*
> (1 Sam. 11:13)

We can applaud Saul's soft heart, but it may be the same compassion that would cause the rulership to be taken away from him. At this point, Samuel suggested they renew the rulership at Gilgal. Now, why did the rulership have to be constantly renewed? What message was being sent—now that Saul had proven himself, we will see what happens next. It seems that Samuel would do anything to stay in the limelight—Samuel did not know how to share leadership. He appeared to support and endorse Saul, but we will see. Saul's reign was marked by wars and rumors of war.

Now with Saul firmly established as ruler, Samuel chose this time to announce his retirement. His "retirement" speech was laced with anger, resentment, and pain. He agreed to continue intercessory prayer for the people but basically told them they were on their own with the new ruler, and Saul began to take center stage.

Saul's reign was marked by war; his reign was bloody as various groups tested his military and administrative leadership. Saul was impressive with the Ammonites, but how did he fare against the dreaded Philistines?

Saul's record was spotty against the Philistines. In the first battle under his leadership, it was not Saul who shined but his son, Jonathan—see 1 Sam. 13:3–4. Samuel told Saul to wait seven days, at which time Samuel would join the troops. But a second attack prompts Saul to summon the troops to Gilgal—where they were totally intimidated by the Philistines. They were so afraid that they hide in caves, holes, rocks, tombs, and cisterns. Some defected into Gad and Gilead; the few that followed Saul did so in fear and trembling. Each day, Saul waited for Samuel and each day more and more men fell away.

With his troops dwindling and Samuel nowhere to be found, Saul took the initiative to save the day—he offered a sacrifice to God. No sooner had he completed the offering than Samuel suddenly appeared. Samuel offered no apology for being late, but he immediately lashed out at Saul. (Read 1 Sam. 13:11–14.)

This is a marked change in how Saul is portrayed—he went from war hero to evil-doer. Saul tried to explain himself but Samuel would not hear of it. Saul was doomed before he even began. In the midst of terrifying circumstances, Saul took action—and was punished for it. It is not clear if the boundary of his power and authority was outlined in the book of rules that Samuel left to Saul and the people. Saul felt that he made the only choice he could—to do anything to enlist God's help against the Philistines. But instead of supporting him, Samuel fired him from his job! Not only was Saul fired, but his replacement was identified. Imagine how this made Saul feel—he didn't get a second chance. He was tried, judged, and convicted in one breath. The whole business raises suspicion—had Saul been set up to fail?

Despite his firing, Saul had to continue with the work at hand—fighting the Philistines. Samuel didn't console Saul, offered no pastoral care, and didn't even offer a prayer for victory. Samuel left Saul to fend for himself. Again, Jonathan shone—he and his armor-bearer waged a surprise attack on the Philistines (see 1 Sam. 14). In the course of his secret mission, Saul called for the ark of God to protect them. The people believed the ark of God, the portable shrine, held the Spirit of God. They felt that God, through the ark, went into battle with them. In this battle, sure enough, they were victorious.

After the victory, Saul laid an oath on the troops:

> *Now Saul committed a very rash act on that day. He had laid an oath on the troops, saying, "Cursed be anyone who eats food before it is evening and I have been avenged on my enemies." So none of the troops tasted food.* (1 Sam. 14:24)

The problem, though, was that everyone heard the oath and adhered to it except Saul's son, Jonathan. So he ate, his eyes brightened, and he knew something had gone terribly wrong. When he learned of his father's oath, Jonathan blamed his father. He said that his father had "troubled" the land. The spiral downward for Saul had begun and it seemed inevitable that Saul would be ousted.

Saul was not willfully evil or bad. He tried to fix the matter by offering to kill his son to redeem the offense of breaking the oath. Saul seemed to be grasping at straws, trying to reassure the people and the priests that he really did respect God. After two "mistakes,"

Saul would do anything to get things back on the right track and save his job. But it was too late. As Saul prepared to murder his son, the people stopped him. (Read 1 Sam. 14:45.)

Saul couldn't win—Samuel overruled his decisions and now the people overruled his decision. The showdown with the Philistines ended in a draw with both armies withdrawing until another time. But Saul was victorious over other enemies—he routed the Moabites, Ammonites, Edomites, Amalekites and others. He even won some minor skirmishes with the Philistines. He exhibited courage and military smarts although the fighting continued. All the fighting had made Saul a bit wiser and he began to develop a standing army of valiant young men (see 1 Sam. 14:52).

Samuel reappeared again to give Saul marching orders against the Amalekites. According to the D tradition, the Amalekites hindered Israel's escape from Egypt and needed to be punished. It was now Saul's job to wipe them out under the banner of "holy war." Saul complied with the command; before attacking the city of the Amalekites, Saul urged the Kenites to leave. The Kenites had been kind to the Israelites when they left Egypt and so deserved mercy. Saul was victorious against the Amalekites, but he did not carry out the *herem*, or ban, by totally destroying the city and all the inhabitants. Saul spared Ruler Agag, the best sheep, cattle, fatlings, and lambs, and all that was valuable. Saul thought that these could be used to sacrifice to God, in gratitude for God's protection.

Samuel and God, however, saw it as more evidence that Saul really didn't have what it took to be ruler. Both Samuel and God reacted negatively to Saul's actions. (Read 1 Sam. 15:10–11.)

Again, Samuel had to bail Saul out of a mess. When Samuel questioned Saul about his actions concerning the Amalekites, Saul told him he had done all that was required. Samuel went ballistic. (Read 1 Sam. 15:13–23.)

This long passage serves as a typical interaction between the two leaders. Saul always respected Samuel and treated him well. Saul harbored no animosity or hostility toward Samuel. He recognizes the wisdom that Samuel embodied and knew that he was a man of God. Samuel, on the other hand, seemed exasperated and impatient with Saul, but it is not clear why. Samuel treated Saul as if he were a little child—a child that was none too bright.

In this incident, Samuel asked a question to which he already knew the answer—he knew that Saul had not completed the *herem*. Samuel made Saul look stupid by asking about the bleating sheep. Before Saul could finish his sentence, Samuel stopped him to interject his assessment of his work. Saul really thought he had followed God's command but Samuel wasn't hearing him. He offered no constructive feedback that would help Saul do a better job. Instead, Samuel fired Saul—again. At that point, Samuel offered information that now made sense to Saul—but why hadn't Samuel told him this earlier?

Saul was a person who took criticism well. He seemed just to want to do a good job. It was not his fault that he simply did not get adequate information. When he recognized the error of his ways, he confessed his "sin" and asked for pardon. In fact, he asked Samuel to go with him so he might worship and ask for God's forgiveness. Saul confessed that he listened to the voice of the people—but what else could he have done? At this point in the story, God had never spoken to Saul directly and Samuel was a usual no-show. Surely Saul felt he was on his own in most matters. The only time Samuel showed up was to criticize, chastise, and humiliate. Even now, Samuel refused to offer pastoral care or compassion. Samuel remained insensitive and mean—instead of agreeing to worship with Saul, Samuel walked away—or he tried to walk away. Saul grabbed the hem of Samuel's garment and tore it. Instead of recognizing Saul's desperation and offering to pray with him, Samuel used the incident as further indictment of Saul's unworthiness. (Read 1 Sam. 15:28–29.)

Not only was Saul once again fired from being ruler, Samuel hurt his feelings further by stating that his replacement was better than Saul! Samuel's treatment of Saul borders on abusive—he used the occasion to make Saul feel like dirt. To make matters worse, Saul knew that he had lost his job but he had not received a termination date—when and where and how was he to leave office? Samuel just kept harping on how worthless Saul was and how his job had been given to another. How much could a person take?

This time, Saul insisted that Samuel treat him with some respect; he was still ruler, after all. Until he was pushed out, Saul still wore the crown. Saul had taken enough public embarrassment from Samuel and the very least he could do was pray with Saul and the people. Samuel relented, especially since he promised the people that he would never stop praying for them. After they worshiped, Samuel completed the *herem* by slaughtering the ruler of the Amalekites. (Read 1 Sam. 15:33–34.)

This points up a glaring contrast between the two men: Saul looked to spare the ruler; Samuel "hewed" him into pieces. Saul offered respect; Samuel humiliated and embarrassed. Saul was contrite and confessed; Samuel was arrogant and chastised. Saul worshiped; Samuel slaughtered. The two men parted ways and each knew that this relationship would never work.

The scene then shifts to focus on David, the ruler elect. But Saul had to continue to move through his days knowing that at any moment his job would be over and that there was someone already standing in the wings ready to take over. Saul lived with this hanging over his head—wouldn't that be enough to drive you crazy? Indeed, we watch as Saul's life unraveled and he was helpless to do anything about it. (Read 1 Sam. 16:14–17.)

Samuel's prophecy came true—the man who became a different person and was anointed with God's Spirit had changed again. God chose and then uninvited Saul. This raises some serious questions about God's judgment—God insisted on choosing Israel's ruler and, while we had questions about Saul (as did those worthless fellows), God seemed confident in the choice. God knows the heart and sees more than we see; God looks beyond outside appearances, although we are told how tall and handsome Saul was—what was

God up to here? And why did God choose Saul, only to let him flounder and fail? Why did God allow Samuel to abuse Saul and make him look foolish and incompetent in public? Why did God and Samuel fail to give Saul a clear job description outlining boundaries and protocol? Why was Saul left to improvise in his new job? So many questions—so little time.

Saul developed a mental condition—and we are not surprised. With the stress in his life and lack of support from those who called him to this job, it's a wonder that Saul survived this long. Unemployment loomed over Saul's head; memories of ill treatment by his boss and a series of demeaning public incidents left Saul wondering what in the world had happened to him. He was living his life, minding his own business, working with his dad, not bothering anyone, and then all of a sudden, things changed. He didn't ask to be ruler, he was commanded. He did his best, and now all he had to show for it are horrible fits of mental fatigue.

To top it all off, the very one assigned to ease his misery with music is none other than his replacement. Unknowingly, Saul invited David into his home—and David was not just a musician—he also was "a man of valor, prudent in speech, a man of good presence, and God was with him." With a description like that, how could Saul refuse to give him a hearing? David was so impressive that Saul embraced him and added him to the inner circle. (Read 1 Sam. 16:21–23.)

I guess there's nothing like a little court intrigue to keep things interesting—Saul, who worried about his job, had invited his successor into his home and his heart. Do you suspect that the storyteller was biased here? Saul was spiraling downward and this David, a keeper of sheep and an upstart, appeared out of nowhere and turned out to be just what the ruler needed?

While Saul dealt with his mental thing, duty called again because the Philistines had reappeared. This time, it was not Jonathan who initiated a defensive response, it was David. David took care of Goliath, the giant of a Philistine (see 1 Sam. 17). In this incident, it seems that Saul had no idea who David was, although the previous passage showed David to be an intimate part of Saul's family. Here, we have evidence of more than one hand in the storytelling. The intrigue builds because Saul apparently didn't yet know David, but Saul's son, Jonathan, loved David (see 1 Sam. 18:1).

Saul sent David out to battle and he was always successful—so much so that the women sang about him. (Read 1 Sam. 18:7–9.)

Saul up to now had shown very little emotion; he was contrite and expressed desperation. But during the times that Samuel had goaded him, Saul had expressed no anger or resentment. Now, Saul was displeased and angry—we see a marked change in his personality. When Saul heard the women singing about the exploits of David, he was jealous and his insecurities began to show. This sets the stage for us to see just how badly Saul had fallen—for the rest of 1 Samuel, Saul and David played a cat-and-mouse game. Saul tried on several occasions to kill David when he was in the ruler's presence, and each time Saul (an expert marksman) missed David (see 1 Sam. 18:10–11 and 19:8–10). Saul's own children worked against him in order to save David's life (see 1 Sam. 18:17–19, 18:20–29, 19:1–7, 19:11–17, 20:1, 23:15–18). Saul, who had been mild-mannered and controlled, began to lash out at his own son for helping David. (Read 1 Sam. 20:30–34.)

Saul was out of control and totally obsessed with killing David—but he could not and would not because David was God's chosen successor. The picture of Saul that emerges from these incidents is quite unflattering. Saul was stark raving mad and there was no possibility of redemption for him.

David had opportunities to kill Saul but chose not to (see 1 Sam. 23:15 and 26:3). We have to question David's motives, though. While he seemed to respect Saul, it may be that David toyed with him—intimidation is a powerful tool. In other words, David might have been playing with Saul to make him look silly, just as Samuel did. Saul seemed to "get it" that David was a good man and deserved to be the next ruler. He gave in and faced reality (see 1 Sam.

24:17–22 and 26:3–25) but his realizations didn't stick. Almost as soon as words of blessing and acceptance left Saul's lips, he was back to pursuing David. Of course, we know that as God's chosen ruler, David would never be killed or even harmed by Saul. The game that ensued between Saul and David would have been funny if it had not so exposed Saul's character flaws.

Saul was the man who didn't want to be ruler; he was out looking for his father's lost donkeys and found a territory. He was a reluctant leader, trying to go back to his old life when duty called. Saul rose to the occasion and proved to be an able warrior. Undergirding his military prowess, however, was a soft heart and a need for approval. When God and Samuel did not support him, he improvised and tried to do the right thing. Samuel, who publicly demeaned him, exposed his misjudgments. When Saul tried to make things right, he was further humiliated and left to his own devices. God withdrew all support and Samuel abandoned Saul. Saul slipped into mental anguish, the only remedy for which was the soothing music that David played. But David turned out to be a formidable enemy who won over the people and Saul's own children. The ruler was a mess and there was nothing he could do about it.

So now, the Philistines were back. There was so much stress in Saul's life. He expended a great deal of time, money, and energy trying to kill David—so much so that he was literally at his wit's end. Things had so spiraled out of control, he just didn't know what to do. He prayed but God didn't answer. Samuel was dead and off the scene (see 1 Sam. 25:1a). Saul cast lots (a method of seeking divine guidance in decision-making), but even the lots were silent. The prophets had nothing constructive or instructive for Saul. Everyone and everything was working against him. Saul saw the handwriting on the wall—it was basically over for him. But he had one last trick up his sleeve.

Early in his reign, Saul had stamped out the practice known as "necromancy," which means consulting the dead for information and help.

Saul had expelled the mediums and the wizards from the land. (1 Sam. 28:3b)

It was a religious move to eliminate the possibility of idolatry. Israel was to depend only on God for everything. But desperate times call for desperate measures. And let's face it, Saul was a desperate man. Saul thought that if he could have one last conversation with Samuel, maybe he would finally get the support he needed. When the Philistines showed up again, Saul was absolutely terrified. He asked his servants to find a medium—even though they had been banished, both Saul and his servants held out the possibility that the practice was an underground activity. And sure enough, a servant knew of a woman in Endor who still practiced.

In the middle of the night and under a disguise, Saul and two of his men made their way to Endor. Saul asked her to consult a dead spirit; at first, she claimed to not know what he wants because the ruler had banished such activity in the land. Saul told her it would be all right if she helped him just this one time. She gave in and, as she began her work, she recognized that Saul was the ruler—the very one who decreed that she could not practice her craft. Saul assured her that he was not there to hurt her; he just needed this one thing. The woman conjured up Samuel—who was not happy about being disturbed.

True to form, Samuel did not help but rather continued to taunt Saul for his incompetence and inability to ride off into the sunset of retirement. Samuel offered no help and this time told Saul that the very next day he and his sons would die. There was no way Saul would win the fight against the Philistines; furthermore, he needed to die so David could become ruler (see 1 Sam. 28:15-19). Saul was shocked and fell over in fear. It was really over now, and death would be almost anticlimactic. Saul had been totally abandoned by God and Samuel. He was haunted by the presence of David, who couldn't wait to be ruler. He had alienated his children. Saul was alone—really and truly alone. But he received comfort from the medium at Endor—she fed him and his servants. It was the last act of kindness that Saul received.

The next day, Saul fought the Philistines on Mount Gilboa and was wounded. His sons, Jonathan, Abinadab, and Malchishua, were killed. Knowing that the end was near, Saul asked his armor-bearer to kill him. The servant refused and Saul had a choice to make. He decided to kill himself. (Read 1 Sam. 31:4–6.)

The Philistines were giddy with delight that they had killed the ruler of Israel. They desecrated Saul's body—beheading him and stripping away his armor. They sent the "good news" throughout their land and put Saul's armor in the temple of their idols. They placed Saul's body on the wall of Beth-shan. The men of Jabesh-gilead (the ones Saul saved in his very first military campaign) retrieved his body, cremated it, and buried his ashes and bones in Jabesh-gilead.

And so ended Saul's reign. Some see his battlefield suicide as a last act of heroism. It was considered dishonorable to die at the hands of the enemy; by taking his own life, Saul avoided that shame. He died valiantly, fighting to the end for his people.

What can we say about Saul and his reign? Scholars are ambivalent, as are the biblical storytellers. Saul was a layered man who could have had it all. But circumstances and people conspired against him and he never got a firm grasp of his mission.

Saul had issues—and his biggest issue revolved around his relationship (or lack of it) with God and Samuel. Neither gave Saul the support and guidance he needed to be effective. Samuel withheld pertinent information, and God had nothing to do with him at all. Saul had to fight war after war with inadequate troops and weapons. Saul had to create an army and equip them but had no help in doing so. He was required to engage in holy wars and completely destroy people and things, all of which offended his sensibilities. He got no relief from the stress of being ruler with no clear job description and no policies or structures in place to guarantee his success. His own children worked against him by loving and supporting David. The very person whose job it was to assist publicly shamed him.

Saul was a pioneer. It is never easy to be the first anything and Saul's story certainly highlights that reality. As the first ruler, Saul had no role models, no mentors, and no examples to follow. He was the transition person and stood in the gap between the old and the new. The one person who understood the stresses and strains of the transition—Samuel—refused to help. And, unfortunately, Saul was not given the option of quitting—he was left on his own and had to do the best he could. His attempts at improvisation are undermined and ridiculed. His main task is to lead the people in war but was easily distracted by his obsession to kill David. He was a warrior and yet was shown time and time again hiding, cowering, and terrified in the face of responsibility. He was God's chosen one, but others outshone him over and over again. He was ruler but was fired from his job when he seemingly overstepped his job boundaries. He sought God's guidance but was ignored—in Saul's whole reign, God never once talked directly to Saul (but talked to David). Saul was a man who stood head and shoulders above the people but died a miserable self-inflicted death on the battlefield.

Saul held great promise, but we will never know what heights he might have reached. From the very beginning, God was ambivalent about appointing a ruler. On the surface, Saul seemed like a good choice—he was from the tribe of Benjamin, a small tribe that was centrally located geographically. The choice did not arouse undue jealousy or suspicion from the other tribes. Saul stood in the tradition of other charismatic leaders (having God's spirit). But at his anointing, he was designated *nagid* rather than *melek*. A *nagid* is a leader or commander of an armed force; *melek* is the Hebrew word for ruler. Perhaps the term *nagid* is used to indicate that God had no intention of actually appointing a ruler; God may have wanted to appoint Saul as a permanent national military leader along the lines of the judges. But clearly the people saw Saul as their ruler and granted him that title.

If God didn't want to appoint a ruler, why didn't God simply refuse the request? God put an evil spirit on Saul and he was helpless to shake it off. Not even soothing music dispelled the spirit. What God did was essentially ruin Saul's life. Because God didn't support him, Saul spiraled into madness. He was isolated and alienated his family, the one place where Saul should have had support and love. If God wanted to teach the people a lesson, why did God use Saul? Samuel's hands were not clean in this matter either—Samuel used every opportunity to shame Saul and expressed little remorse about his actions. He provided little understanding or compassion for Saul's situation.

Saul did not make sweeping changes in Israel—he did not build a fabulous palace or accumulate a harem or group of concubines. He barely established an army and had only a modest cabinet of leaders. He did not establish a royal bureaucracy. But Saul was clearly popular, garnered loyalty from those who followed him, and was courageous and willing to admit his faults. At the same time, he became increasingly jealous and paranoid. He exhibited wild mood swings and became obsessed with killing David. He was temperamental and was not above resorting to brutal violence (see 1 Sam. 21:1–9 and 22:9–19). The cards were stacked against Saul from the very beginning. He was never able to wipe out the Philistine threat and he never established unity and harmony among the tribes. He was asked to do an impossible job and was penalized when he fails. It seems that both God and Samuel have some explaining to do when it comes to Saul. And we are left to ponder the roles that God and Samuel played in Saul's demise.

REFLECTION QUESTIONS

1. Describe a time when you were the "new kid on the block" either at school or work. What would have helped you feel welcomed?

2. Have you ever been in a situation where someone tried to sabotage your leadership? Explain.

3. Saul has personal challenges and concerns. Does your personal life interfere with your ability to be a good leader? Explain.

4. Do you consider yourself to be a leader? Explain your response.

5. From where do you find support for your leadership? With whom do you discuss leadership concerns?

6. What are Saul's leadership strengths? What are his leadership weaknesses?

7. What advice would you offer Saul about his leadership?

8. How important is self-care for leaders? How do you take care of yourself? Are your current practices adequate to sustain you?

9. List the major stressors for leaders. What can be done to ease the leadership strain?

10. Have you ever been fired? How did you deal with the situation?

3 · DAVID

WHO'S THE MAN? I'M THE MAN!

Read 2 Samuel 5:1–6, 7:11–17

So we finally come to the man of the hour: David. No other figure looms as large on the biblical scene as does David. Certainly we get a lot of Moses, Abraham, and Jacob—but word for word, none gets the press that David does. He sets the standard by which all rulers of Israel are measured. So we would expect a man of impeccable character and focus. The reality, however, is very different from the ideal.

David was the second ruler of Israel and had the benefit of reflecting on Saul's reign. The job of ruler was becoming clearer and David was at a decided advantage over Saul who had no blueprint to follow. David, the man after God's own heart, is portrayed as the ideal ruler. When the people longed for a redeemer during Jesus' day, they used David as the symbol of needed characteristics—pious, faithful, courageous, smart, sincere, competent—simply wonderful. But as we will see, David had his own issues and foibles.

David was one of the biggest personalities in the Bible. Unfortunately, we are not able to go into detail on his life and leadership. We will look at just a few episodes of his reign. Many books and articles have been written about him and almost all of them are complimentary. We will study a few incidents to see if he merits the accolades from biblical storytellers and modern biblical scholars.

We hear about David long before we actually meet him in scripture. His arrival was foretold shortly after Saul assumes the rulership. He was an unlikely successor to Saul. In 1 Samuel 16, we find Samuel grieving over Saul's decline. God had no patience with Samuel and admonished him to be done with his grief. God commanded Samuel to go to Bethlehem to anoint the ruler-elect, the youngest son of Jesse. Samuel, again, was amazed at God's choice but followed God's order. David was ruddy, had beautiful eyes, and was handsome. It seems that God had a preference for handsome men. David was anointed in the presence of his father and his brothers; God's Spirit rested on David (see 1 Sam. 16:13).

We next see David when he joined the court of Saul. David's reputation as a musician and singer was widespread. David was the musician who soothed the ruler's moments of distress and pain (1 Sam. 16:14–23); in the next chapter, however, we "meet" David again, as if chapter 16 does not exist. In 1 Samuel 17, we find the familiar story of David and Goliath. David, young, unequipped, precocious, and brave, fought Goliath and won a victory for Israel over the Philistines. Everyone was impressed, including Saul's son, Jonathan, who developed a special friendship with David. Saul sent David out on more military expeditions and David was always victorious. Saul put David in charge of the army and all seemed well and right in Saul's court—that is, until the women started singing David's praises. Although Saul was the ruler, David was the man!

David was quite impressive and both men and women loved him. He seemed to take this adulation, admiration, and attention in stride. He went about his business, doing what he was told without complaining or resisting. I imagine that David learned as much as he could and would use what he learned to his advantage when the opportunity presented itself. He moved through Saul's plots to kill him, always escaping unharmed. David seemed to be the innocent victim of Saul's envy, anger, and resentment. Saul's own children defied their father to assist David. David accepted their help and seemed bewildered by Saul's actions. In fact, David seemed to look up to Saul with respect and deference. When Saul offered his oldest daughter, Merab, in marriage, David pretended that he was not worthy to be the ruler's son-in-law. David offered the same sentiment when he was offered Saul's younger daughter, Michal (see 1 Sam. 18:18, 23). David conveyed humility in the face of the offers, but he was smart enough to realize that such marriages would benefit him politically. Even Jonathan went out of his way to keep David safe; at one point, Jonathan bore the brunt of his father's rage about David.

Early in his career with Saul, David is depicted as a man on the run—he was constantly outwitting Saul as the ruler chased him around the country (see 1 Sam. 19:18; 20:1–3; 21:10–15; 22:1–5; 23:13–14, 25–29; 24:1–3; 27:1–4). The movement was circuitous and almost comical. No matter what Saul did, David maintained the upper hand. We are tempted to feel sorry for David but we must also question his motives. David took Saul on a wild goose chase that made him look foolish. David did to Saul what Samuel had done—placed him in situations where Saul was clearly the loser. David was a smart, ambitious person and calculated his moves.

As David tried to stay out of the clutches of Saul, we see aspects of his personality that make us wonder what he was up to. David knew how to wheel and deal and was not above deception if it suited his purposes. He lied to Ahimelech, the priest at Nob (see 1 Sam. 21:1–6) who gives him sanctuary, food, water, and Goliath's sword that Saul had taken. As a result of assisting David, Ahimelech and the priests with him were brutally murdered by Saul (see 1 Sam. 22:11–19).

As he ventured into the territory of King Achish of Gath, David pretended to be crazy to escape harm. (Read 1 Sam. 21:12–15.) When David went to his native Judah, he found support. Even the "worthless" fellows attached themselves to David. His posse consisted of malcontents, fugitives, thugs, and outlaws. It is likely that even his relatives joined his band; we will keep an eye on David's nephews Joab, Abishai, and Asahel, who exhibit quite violent tendencies that worked to David's advantage, too. David became the leader of a gang; yes, David was a gang-banger and established a private military force. (Read 1 Sam. 22:1–3.)

David lived the life of a bandit or outlaw—he attacked the Philistines when it was expedient; he collected protection money from the wealthy in exchange for his military skills; and at the same time he managed to dodge Saul's advances. Saul said that David was "very cunning" (1 Sam. 23:22) and that is an apt description. David knew how to play both ends against the middle and all to his advantage. Even his marriages were politically advantageous; he married Ahinoam of Jezreel and Abigail the widow of Nabal of Carmel (see 1 Sam. 25:43–44)—both from important families in the south.

David, however, soon found himself caught between a rock and a hard place—on the run from Saul, constantly watching for the Philistines, and being snitched on by Saul's spies. David made a bold and calculating move by offering to serve King Achish in Philistine territory. (Read 1 Sam. 27:5–7.)

It appears that David was a traitor and had defected to the side of Israel's enemy. But sly David gave King Achish false reports that he was attacking territory in Judah when he was actually attacking the Amalekites and other neighboring cities and towns. He took the spoils of these raids and gave them to his kinfolk throughout Judah. This solidified their loyalty to David and served as hush money to keep his covert operation a secret. At the same time, Achish thought he had an ally and loyal servant in David. Achish trusted David and considered him an important part of his court (see 1 Sam. 27:8–12). When the Philistines geared up to attack Israel again, they refused David's help although it would have placed David in an interesting position—would he blow his cover and fight with Israel or would he betray his country by joining the Philistines in their war against Israel? David never had to choose—another sign that God was with him. (Read 1 Sam. 29:6–11.)

David was a good actor and played his role well; lucky for him the decision to exclude him from the attack on Israel had already been made. The battle did not go well for Israel and Saul and his three sons died in battle. Once again, Israel found itself in dire straits. In fact, the rulership experiment appeared to be a dismal failure—the nation was worse off now than they were before calling Saul as ruler. The Philistines recaptured territories that Israel had taken. Not only had Israel lost ground, their ruler was dead. There were no policies governing the line of succession. Some assumed that one of Saul's surviving sons would rule; others looked for another leader. The way was clear for David to assume the rulership.

The book of 2 Samuel focuses on David's reign. As the book opens, Saul and his sons have died in the battle against the Philistines. David led a time of national mourning for the dead ruler. David seemed sincere in his grief and certainly paid public respect fitting the first ruler of Israel. David's kin people wanted him to be ruler. With the full consent of God, David went to Hebron, where he was anointed ruler. (Read 2 Sam. 2:1–4.)

We assume that David's anointing has the approval of the Philistines; at this point, David still worked for them. The Philistines, no doubt, were pleased because they could add Judah to their list of territories. They trusted David and probably celebrated this turn of events.

David followed in Saul's footsteps in that he, too, was a gifted military leader. He was the hometown son who had done well for himself. In addition, David commanded a strong personal army. The elders of Judah felt confident that David would protect them and intervene, if needed, with the Philistines. They apparently made David ruler without consulting any of the other tribes. This did not bode well for Israel. But life was good all the way around—or so it seemed.

David was different from Saul in some important ways. The differences mark a step away from the old patterns that Samuel tried so hard to keep alive. First, David was a veteran warrior. Saul became ruler as he was looking for his father's lost donkeys. David had an impressive list of military victories already under his belt. He had proven that he was able to go up against giants and emerge a winner. Second, David already had a standing army of sorts—his renegade gang members form his personal armed force. Saul tried to establish an army by selecting valiant young men into his service, David was among them. But David's posse numbered in the hundreds and was a force with which others had to reckon. Third, David had gained valuable administrative experience under the tutelage of the Philistines, who had given him territory to govern. Saul came into the job without any experience or notions about how to govern. David had been tutored by the best. David was well equipped to take on the rulership and he was more than ready.

In an effort to either show support for Saul's memory or to make sure there were no sons of Saul still living, David sent word of his anointing to the people of Jabesh-gilead who had given Saul a suitable burial. The word he got back was surprising—David might be ruler over Judah, but Israel had a ruler from Saul's house, Ishbaal (Ish-bosheth). The simmering hostility between Judah (in the south) and Israel (in the north) reached the boiling point, and all-out war broke out between them. Sadly, this dispute highlighted Saul's inability to fully unite the tribes—now there were two "states" vying for superiority and power—Israel and Judah.

In the war between the two states, Abner led the troops of Saul and Joab led David's troops. In the first encounter, David and Joab were decisively victorious. Ishbaal and Abner were embarrassed. Abner was chased by one of David's soldiers, Asahel, who also happened to be David's nephew and Joab's brother. In a surprising move, Abner killed Asahel (see 2 Sam. 2:18–23). Joab and his brother Abishai then tried to catch Abner but he eluded them.

David, ever the diplomat, did not want to widen the gap between Judah and Israel. He did not order a contract on Abner to avenge his nephew's murder. The stage was set, though, for more bloodshed because Joab would not let the matter rest. In the meantime, we see that Ishbaal was more a figurehead than a real threat to David. It seems that Abner was the real powerhouse in Israel. When Ishbaal accused Abner of seeking the crown for himself (it was rumored that Abner wanted one of Saul's concubines, a clear indication of ambition to the throne), Abner renounced his allegiance to Ishbaal and Saul's house. Abner switched teams and threw his support to David. Not only that, Abner urged the elders of Israel to go over to David's side.

David welcomed the overture with one request—that his wife, Michal, Saul's daughter, be returned to him. This caused some angst because Saul took her away from David and married her off to another man. But Ishbaal ordered her to go to David—David's wishes had already caused problems for families. We can see this as a foreshadowing of his realationship with Bathsheba. (Read 2 Sam. 3:14–16.)

At Abner's urging, the elders of Israel rushed to support David. But when Joab heard of the agreement between Abner and David, he was livid. He accused Abner of trying to set David up for defeat, but David was not convinced. Joab went after Abner and murdered him to avenge his brother's death (see 2 Sam. 3:26–27). When David learned that Abner has been killed, he immediately shifted into public relations mode—he made sure that his hands were clean. He placed the blame on Joab and called for a time of national mourning for the former commander-in-chief. David put on a good public show for the sake of the Israelites and encouraged Joab to do the same. (Read 2 Sam. 3:31–32.)

David was convincing—he refused to eat, so deep was his grief over Abner. While the house of Saul was getting weaker, David was getting stronger. The people bought his act hook, line, and sinker:

All the people took notice of it, and it pleased them; just as everything the ruler did pleased all the people. (2 Sam. 3:36)

In addition to erasing any thoughts that he was implicated in Abner's death, David made sure that others knew that he was not ordering such violence. Remember that David's personal army or posse was made up renegade malcontents. They had roamed the countryside with David, fighting and killing. Now suddenly, David had a "problem" with the men who made up his gang, especially Joab. He even intimated that he did not condone violence and simply could not control his men:

> *Today I am powerless, even though anointed ruler;*
> *these men, the sons of Zeruiah, are too violent for me.*
> *[YHWH] pay back the one who does wickedly in*
> *accordance with his wickedness!" (2 Sam. 3:39)*

And if you believe that, I have some prime real estate—swamp land—for your consideration! The issue is that Joab and David were linked—they needed each other if David was to build a strong empire. David was the brain and Joab was the brawn—both had brains and brawn and the two made a formidable duo. Things got complicated because they knew each other so well. Although David claimed he was distressed by Joab's actions, he did not punish him nor did David dismiss him from his service. And, truth be told, Joab's murder of Abner worked to David's political advantage and to Joab's military advantage—it was a win-win situation for them. David was rid of an enemy and possible contender to the throne (Abner was Saul's cousin). Joab was rid of a potential aspirant to the commander-in-chief position that Joab currently occupied. That Joab was silent in the face of David's rebuke is interesting to note.

Shortly after Abner's death, Ishbaal died at the hands of two of his officers. The men brought Ishbaal's head to David expecting the ruler to be pleased. However, David stayed true to form and refused to reward the men; instead, David had them killed. Again, he was able to convince the people that he had not played a part in Ishbaal's demise. So convinced were the people that they gathered en masse in Hebron to declare David the ruler of "all Israel" (read 2 Sam.

5:1–3). With this act, David now represented the unity of Israel and Judah. The new "state" was on shaky ground, but for the time being the two entities were united in the person of King David. This act also widened the gap between the old ways of the tribal league and the new ways of the monarchy.

Tension between those loyal to Saul and those now loyal to David never quite dissipated. David worked hard to bring healing—he even hoped that the return of Michal, Saul's daughter promised to him in marriage, would further the healing process.

But David had other problems brewing. Remember that he was still employed by the Philistines. When David was declared ruler of all Israel, it was a signal to the Philistines that David had broken away and formed his own rival territory. David also understood that the move would be seen as a declaration of independence from Philistine domination. David was also smart enough to realize that the Philistines would not simply let him go—they would do whatever it took to keep David under their control.

In a brilliant move (only one of many), David and his posse led by Joab marched into Jebusite territory. The Jebusites were a group of Canaanites occupying the central area. David took Jerusalem, and made some remarkable moves. He claimed the city for himself and Jerusalem (or Zion) became known as the City of David; because he used his personal army to take the city, it belonged to the crown and not to the tribes. He moved his capital city from Hebron to Jerusalem. Jerusalem was neutral territory that neither Israel nor Judah could lay claim to; David established his power base and legacy in one fell swoop. He could not have made this move without the military prowess of his trusty sidekick, Joab. Because Joab watched his back, David was able to establish his royal court—he moved his wives, concubines, and children to Jerusalem.

This was too much for the Philistines to bear—David was amassing power and land. He had to be stopped by any means necessary. The Philistines began their quest to destroy David. Of course, David had a plan that he worked to perfection. First, he sought God's guidance and blessing, which God granted (remember that God was silent with Saul)—read 2 Sam. 5:19. David, with the help of Joab, was successful in warding off the Philistines. But they would not take defeat, and they struck again (see 2 Sam. 5:22–25). David again sought God's guidance—God commanded him to strike from the rear, which David did, and he was again successful. From this point on, the Philistine threat disappeared and some of the Philistines joined David's army. David accepted them, an indication of his inclusive policy. He embraced those who were loyal to him and his administration. No doubt he and Joab taught the men how to be good soldiers.

David had thus proven his military and political acumen—he was definitely the man! He had overcome his enemies and established himself in a new capital city. He built a magnificent palace. There was yet another thing he must do—gain religious support for his reign. David did this by bringing the ark of God to Jerusalem. You will remember that the ark resided in Kirjath-jearim after one of Saul's early battles. David transferred the ark with grand celebration, pomp, and circumstance. He led the celebration and even offered burnt offerings and sacrifices and lifted up a blessing for the occasion. Because David was a musician, it was within reason for him to lead the way. And he got totally into the spirit of the event— see 2 Sam. 6:12–19. It is interesting to note that David performed priestly acts and was not chastised for it. While Saul lost his job for overstepping his bounds, David was praised for his priestly acts. But not everyone was happy with his behavior.

David's wife, Michal, was appalled and disgusted with David's display of pure joy. She was totally turned off by his dancing, shouting, singing, and joyous celebration. She may have been looking for any excuse to bring David down; perhaps she preferred her previous life with her husband to being one of David's many women. Whatever her motivation, Michal let David know in no uncertain terms that she was not pleased. She thought he should behave in a manner befitting his position. David let her know that he was the ruler and he would rejoice wholeheartedly in front of God. (Read 2 Sam. 6:21–22.)

And David didn't care who saw him and what they thought. David danced for God and nothing was gong to stop him—not even the disapproval of a wife. In fact, if she had any sense of God's awesome power and splendor, she would be dancing, too. Michal's reward for criticizing David's action was childlessness.

David had completely changed Israel and solidified his power base:

- He exercised political power by establishing his capital at Jerusalem.
- He exercised military power by overcoming his enemies and gaining new territory (see 2 Sam. 8).
- He made extensive use of his personal army and gave Joab much authority as commander-in-chief.
- He exercised spiritual power by bringing the ark to Jerusalem and by appointing the priests Abiathar and Zadok as co-priests in the capital city.
- He exercised economic power by collecting tribute from subject peoples and adding the spoils of war to the state treasury.
- He exercised labor power by enlisting subject people for his state army and to complete his building projects.
- He established a cabinet of leaders that included a commander of the army, a recorder, a secretary, a leader of subject peoples, and two priests (see 2 Sam. 8:15–17).

David did a masterful job linking the old order to the new order—the territory was distinctively his. He took control of territories held by the Philistines, Moabites, Arameans, Edomites, Ammonites, and Amalekites, among others. Through it all, David was loved, adored, and respected:

So David reigned over all Israel; and David administered justice and equity to all his people. (2 Sam. 8:15)

The one thing that would complete his takeover of Israel was to build a fitting temple to God. He asked the prophet Nathan if he should; Nathan gave his consent at first. But God corrected the prophet. (Read 2 Sam. 7:5–9.)

David would not build a house for God, but God established a house for David—the Davidic dynasty was in effect! Things were going extremely well for David and he was smart enough to keep it that way. He worked to make sure there were no surprise threats to his territory:

> *David asked, "Is there still anyone left of the house of*
> *Saul to whom I may show kindness for Jonathan's sake?"*
> (2 Sam. 9:1)

David wanted to honor his oath to Jonathan, certainly. But it was also likely that he wanted to make sure that there were no other relatives of Saul who could either lay claim to the crown or start a rebellion against him. Remember that David was smart and cunning. David learned that Jonathan's son, who had a disability, was living in Lo-debar. David sent for Mephibosheth, who paid obeisance to David. David extended hospitality and kindness to Jonathan's son. Most likely David was motivated by a sense of obligation to the oath between Jonathan and himself (see 1 Sam. 18:1–4, 20:14–17). I am sure that David was sincere in making a place for Mephibosheth and his family in Jerusalem—but how convenient to have a surviving contender to the throne so close by and so beholden to him. Mephibosheth had a young son, Mica—the house of Saul was declining but was not yet dead.

We will end this section with a little more attention to the intertwining destinies of David and his commander-in-chief, Joab. None of David's military exploits would have been successful without the able assistance of Joab, David's nephew. Remember that when David was on the run from Saul, he gathered a group of roughnecks who raided the countryside with him. David was no angel and was not above killing his opponents—for just cause in most cases.

David's life was marked by violence and he seemed to enjoy the drama surrounding his exploits. It is not conceivable, therefore, that his posse would have been composed of peace-loving men. Rather, his gang members reflected David's own personality. David was too smart to hang out with dummies. It was likely that Joab joined David's band of outlaws early on and rose in rank. Together, David and Joab plotted, schemed, maimed, murdered, and won battles.

David was just another warrior without Joab; with him, David was formidable and invincible. Together they were a force with which others had to reckon. Their relationship required complete trust and confidence in the other. Yet there was something going on with the two of them that bubbled just below the surface.

The tension is hinted at in an incident with the Ammonites—read 2 Sam. 10. David learned that the ruler of the Ammonites had died, and he sent his condolences through a corps of ambassadors. But the Ammonites remembered that David was clever and cunning and they were suspicious. (Read 2 Sam. 10:3.)

Hanun, the new ruler of the Ammonites, embarrassed David's men by cutting their beards and their garments and sending them away. When David found out about this, he had no choice but to deal severely with the Ammonites. King Hanun realized the error of his ways and began mobilizing troops to defend himself against the wrath of David. He hired the Arameans of Beth-rehob and Zobah and formed a coalition with the ruler of Maacah and the men of Tob—he collected massive support.

David simply ordered Joab to handle the situation, which he did brilliantly; not only was Joab an able warrior, he also inspired and encouraged the troops:

> *Be strong, and let us be courageous for the sake of our*
> *people, and for the cities of our God; and may [YHWH]*
> *do what seems good. (2 Sam. 10:12)*

David joined the fight and was victorious. But the credit for the victory went to Joab and his brilliant strategy (read 2 Sam.

10:7–19). David and Joab were mirror images of each other—both were smart, courageous, valiant, fearless, ruthless when needed, and pious. They were complicit in the war crimes they committed; they knew each other's secrets. They trusted each other in guarded ways. They needed each other in order to reach their goals and be successful. As we see in the next section, Joab would play a major role in David's family life. David would use him when it was convenient and expedient to do so. Joab was a loyal follower of David—it will be interesting to see how their relation developed.

REFLECTION QUESTIONS

1. What kind of leader was David? How do you feel about the violence that David dished out?

2. What are David's leadership strengths and weaknesses so far?

3. Do you think David was sincere in his laments about Saul, Jonathan and Abner? Explain.

4. How do you rate David's administrative skills? Explain.

5. Does the end justify the means or do means justify the end? Explain.

6. Did David operate out of self-interest or did he work for the common good?

7. How does an ambitious person live an ethical life? How ambitious are you? How do you keep your ambition in control?

8. What advice would you offer David about his relationship with Joab?

9. How did David deal with conflict?

10. Why did God love David so much? Do you feel loved by God? Explain.

4 · DAVID

THIS IS MY HOUSE, FOREVER AND EVER!

Read 2 Samuel 11:1–27; 1 Kings 1:1–4

David, savvy warrior and politician, suddenly lost interest in fighting. That was the beginning of his decline—and it was pretty nasty stuff. His personal life suddenly took center stage. The picture is none too pretty but reveals just how human David was. Even though he was ruler and the man after God's own heart, David, too, had to live with the consequences of his choices and decisions. Unlike Saul, God didn't fire him from his job as ruler—the matter was curious, to say the least.

With the opening verses of 2 Samuel 11, we detect a turning point in David's reign and his life, and the storyteller makes a telling remark. (Read 2 Sam. 11:1.)

David, the warrior ruler, stayed behind in Jerusalem while his troops trotted off to fight. We are not told why David stayed behind, but we surmise that nothing good would come from his self-imposed vacation. And the story that unfolds is one with tragic dimensions. Until this point, we have seen very little of David's personal life. We saw him on the battlefield, we saw him building his empire, we saw him power-brokering with other powerful men. We know that he was married and also had a large harem. We know that he had children but we didn't see much of what happened behind closed doors. Now his life is laid out for our scrutiny.

David used poor judgment when he gave in to his lust for Bathsheba. His voyeurism landed him in deep trouble when she announced she was pregnant. Under the law, David's act of adultery was punishable by death. (Read Deut. 22:22.)

The ruler of all Israel, so savvy in political and military matters, thus compromised his reign and his life by giving in to his libido. He used his royal prerogative to have sex with another man's wife. It is popular to suggest that Bathsheba seduced David and to blame her for the repercussions of their act. Some scholars have read the text in this manner. However, the responsibility of the act fell squarely on David's shoulder. He was a peeping Tom who boldly watched the woman bathe. He exercised no discretion in the matter and just as boldly sent men to bring her to him. It was not within her right to refuse an audience with the ruler—she had to go when summoned. Also, it was not within her right to refuse his sexual advancements. Some suggest that Bathsheba somehow knew that the king had not gone off to war and that he had a direct view of her roof from the palace.

They suggest that she deliberately timed her bath so he noticed her. She hoped that he would send for her, knowing that her husband was away at war. It is also suggested that Bathsheba sought a liaison with David so she could have a child; apparently, she was childless with her husband. At any rate, probably nothing more would have been made of the incident had not Bathsheba become pregnant (which was her plan all along, according to some readings of the text). I contend that whatever her motivations (if any), David was a powerful man who got his way, regardless. He used his royal privilege and his power as a man in a patriarchal society to have his way with the wife of another man. We know she was not the first married woman David took—remember Abigail and Michal.

As far as we know, David was okay with indulging in a one-night stand and sending the woman back to her life. No one would know of his deed. David was not interested in developing a relationship with Bathsheba, had no interest in getting to know her better, and would not gain politically from a liaison with her. She was convenient and once he had his way with her, she was to go back to her life and keep her mouth shut. In reality, David offered no apology and showed no remorse for violating her. And there is no question that David was the father of the child—the text states clearly that Bathsheba had just ended her menstrual cycle: "Now she was purifying herself after her period" (2 Sam. 11:4b).

In an effort to save his life, and hers, David plotted a cover-up that failed—he orders Joab, his trusted commander, to send Uriah home. David hoped that Uriah would have sex with his wife and thus claim the child as his own. David went to great lengths to set up Uriah, but Uriah unwittingly did not play along with the plot. So David felt he had no choice but to make sure Uriah died in battle. He implicated Joab in his plot. Ironically, David sent a letter to Joab with Uriah, who unknowingly carried his own death warrant. Joab didn't ask any questions about David's sudden interest in Uriah or why he wanted Uriah dead—Joab followed orders. When news of Uriah's demise reached David, he sent a message to Joab that further tied them together in intrigue. (Read 2 Sam. 11:25.)

In other words, war brought unavoidable collateral damage. David set up Uriah to be killed and implicated Joab in his war crime. In addition to Uriah, other innocent soldiers were killed to cover up David's deed. David had overstepped the bounds of his power. But according to David, that's just the way it is sometimes.

When Bathsheba learned her husband was dead, she mourned. Shortly after that, David married her and she gave birth to a son. It seemed as though David had gotten away with murder and adultery—long live the king!

But God had something to say about the matter:

> *But the thing that David had done displeased [YHWH], and [YHWH] sent Nathan to David. (2 Sam. 11:27b)*

The prophet Nathan had a story to tell David (read 2 Sam. 12:1–12). Nathan rebuked David. Interestingly, David was chastised but he was not killed nor did he lose his job for this sin (remember Saul was promptly fired by Samuel). But David had a troubled personal life to look forward to because of his indiscretion. Furthermore, the child of his lust paid the cost for David's act—with his life. (Read 2 Sam. 12:15a–18.)

The death of the child seems especially cruel and unjust, given that God sanctioned it. The judgment against David was expunged as a sign that David was God's special servant. For the shapers of the tradition, it was God's right to give life and to take it away. We want to hold God responsible for the senseless death of the innocent child. But in this case, there were no words to save the child.

While David was handling, or rather mishandling, his domestic affairs, Joab was taking care of business on the battlefield. He was successful against the Ammonites—without David. But Joab knew the king was at his best when fighting. Joab sent a pointed message to David—either come to the scene of the action or Joab would take Rabbah and name it after himself (see 2 Sam. 12:27–28). Joab's ultimatum jarred David back to reality and he got back to business. Not only did David take the city, he also put the spoils of war and the captured people to good use as laborers.

After some time had passed, palace intrigue again reared its ugly head. This time, David's daughter, Tamar, was raped by her half-brother, Amnon. It was a violent and sordid deed—Amnon was smitten by his sister's beauty and fell in love with her. He en-

listed the help of his crafty cousin, Jonadab, to get Tamar. Amnon
pretended to be sick. When David checked on him, Amnon asked
David to send Tamar to nurse him. An unsuspecting David allowed
Tamar to tend to her half-brother. Once he had her alone in his
room, Amnon made his intentions known. She protested that he
wanted to do something forbidden in Israel, something vile. She let
him know that they both would pay a high price for a moment of
passion. But if he talked to David, who certainly understood about
the power of lust, David might allow them the relationship. Amnon
refused to listen and overpowered her. The Hebrew word that is
translated "forced" (2 Sam. 13:14) implies a sexually exploitative act
of the strong over the weak and is especially violent.

As suddenly as he had fallen in love with her, he now loathed
her and ordered her to leave. We are not told the reason for the sudden change in his feelings for her. He was in love with her when she
was unattainable. He burned with love for her from afar. But as soon
as his lust was satisfied, he had no further use for her. He loathed
her—hated her with great hatred—and insisted that she leave. His
actions mirrored David's toward Bathsheba. We don't know if David
forced Bathsheba, but he certainly felt no need to keep her around
once his lust was sated.

Tamar protested the treatment from Amnon, but he had her
forcibly removed from his room. (Read 2 Sam. 13:15b–17.)

But Tamar did not let the matter die quietly. Her half-brother
had violated her twice—first by raping her and secondly by refusing
to marry her (the practice was later forbidden in Israel). She grieved
the loss of her virginity in public:

> *But Tamar put ashes on her head, and tore the long robe*
> *that she was wearing; she put her hand on her head, and*
> *went away, crying aloud as she went. (2 Sam. 13:19)*

Amnon, unlike David, was unable to cover up his crime.
Tamar refused to be a mere pawn in Amnon's lustful game. She was
a smart woman, verbal, thoughtful, and convincing in her argument.

She spoke her mind and, when Amnon tried to silence and dismiss her, she found a way to hold him accountable for his violation of her. Her brother Absalom tried to console her, but she was nothing more than damaged goods and was destined to live forever in her brother's house. The victim was thus further victimized by Amnon's violent act.

When David learned of the deed, he was very angry, but it is not clear what David was angry about or at whom. Usually quite articulate and decisive, David here did not say a word and took no action on his daughter's behalf (see 2 Sam. 13:21).

The ruler, who had committed a similar violation and should have understood consequences, did nothing. He didn't talk to Amnon nor did he comfort Tamar. David, who always had a plan, seemed helpless to take care of his family business. But Absalom harbored anger and hatred towards his half-brother.

That anger and hatred simmered and festered for two years before Absalom took action on behalf of his sister. Absalom manipulated David so he allowed Amnon and all his brothers to join Absalom with the sheepshearers at Baal-hazor for a feast. David asked why but didn't press the matter and gave in to Absalom's request. For David, the nasty business between Amnon and Tamar and Absalom was in the past. Remember that David thought his nasty business with Bathsheba was over when he sent her home from his room that afternoon.

Both David and Amnon underestimated Absalom's creativity, patience, and thirst for revenge. Amnon showed up at the feast without a worry or concern for his safety. But Absalom had designed a plot to kill Amnon. Absalom's servants did the deed, just as Joab did a similar deed for David. Absalom had had time to carefully construct a plan. Perhaps he had daydreamed and fantasized about avenging the violation against his sister. No doubt he watched Tamar day after day living with the shame of sexual abuse hanging over her head. At any rate, at the appointed time, in the midst of a party, Absalom's servant struck and killed Amnon.

Understandably, pandemonium broke out; everyone fled to save himself. Absalom had taken care of the business David chose to ignore. Absalom showed that he was patient yet ruthless. Not only had he helped his sister, he also had cleared the way for him to take the throne. Amnon's death made Absalom the oldest living son and next in line to be ruler—was he his father's son or what?

The initial report that David received erroneously states that Absalom had killed all David's sons. David believes the report and freaks out:

> *The king rose, tore his garments, and lay on the ground; and all his servants who were standing by tore their garments. (2 Sam. 13:31)*

If the report was true, David's hope for an everlasting dynasty was dead in one act of brutality. Maybe David regretted not taking a more active parental role with his sons. Maybe David thought Absalom was coming after him. Jonadab, who had helped Amnon pull off the rape, brought an accurate account to David. He made it clear to David that Absalom killed only Amnon to avenge the shame brought on Tamar. We are not told how Jonadab knew Absalom's motivation—the bottom line, though, was that Amnon was dead.

Before David could deal with the situation, Absalom fled (see 2 Sam. 13:34, 37–38). Absalom might have run for a number of reasons—to avoid facing David, to hide from any of Amnon's allies seeking to avenge his assassination, to save his life from David's possible wrath. Just as David was a man on the run from Saul, Absalom was on the run from David.

David grieved and must have been shocked at this turn of events. One day, things seemed to be moving right along, and the next, there was nothing but chaos and turmoil. The words of the prophet Nathan were sinking in and filling David with dread.

David yearned for the lost Absalom and it distracted him from his work. David was probably depressed over his family life. Three years later, Absalom was still in exile and David had not recovered. It is not clear why David didn't go after Absalom or send someone to bring him home. Although Absalom was an assassin and murderer of his brother, he was still David's beloved son and heir to the throne.

At the same time, we wonder what Absalom was up to; apparently he was making no move to return home. We don't know if his mother or sister communicated with him. We know he was a patient, long-suffering person. We may find out later about his activities in exile, but for now, we are clueless.

It is interesting to note God's absence and silence in these texts. Early in David's career, he and God were best buddies. David didn't make a move without checking with God. God never tired of David's inquiries and was more than willing to lead and guide David. Now God is totally absent from the narrative. When David stayed in Jerusalem at the time that rulers go out to war, his whole life changed. David did not consult with God about his decision to have Bathsheba. He certainly did not ask God how to cover up his sin against Uriah. David, so superior to Saul, was now like him, with no direct communication or intimacy with God. Just as God had spoken to Saul through Samuel, God now spoke to David through others. David's one misguided act of indiscretion played out in horrible family drama—one child dead in infancy; a daughter raped, shamed, and humiliated by her half-brother; oldest son a sexual abuser and now dead; second son a murderer and in exile. There was nothing but blood on David's hands and he watched his children suffer for his crimes.

It seems that Israel's experiment with rulership fared no better under David. The man after God's own heart was a whimpering, pitiful sight as he grieved over his family mess—long live the king!

A picture of a depressed, listless David is disturbing to us. So imagine Joab's reaction. Joab had probably been holding the territory together and recognized that David needed to be shocked back into action—so, he took charge.

Joab conspired with an unnamed wise woman from Tekoa— read 2 Sam. 14:1–16. Joab asked her to pretend to be a grieving mother of two sons. She sought the ruler's advice on what to do with the murderous son—she yearned for him despite his crime. Her interaction with David, orchestrated by Joab, served its purpose: David ordered his exiled son home.

Joab gladly went to get Absalom. Joab acted in David's best interest. This incident shows the kind of relationship David and Joab shared. Both were warriors and could be ruthless. Both were shrewd, clever, and cunning. Both were men of action. Joab certainly understood human nature and did whatever was needed to bring David out of the doldrums. Again, David would not have been the man he was without Joab. Joab always showed David the utmost respect, even though David never publicly acknowledged Joab's loyalty or ability.

Although David allowed Absalom to come home, he did so with conditions. David didn't want to see him. David had not quite yet forgiven Absalom even though he yearned for him. Such ambivalence was different for David. He was usually pragmatic, decisive, and headstrong. We now see a different picture of him as cold, stubborn, unbending; in this way, he reminds us of Samuel. David allowed Absalom to come home but kept him at arm's length. How long could this situation last?

> *So Absalom lived two full years in Jerusalem, without coming into the ruler's presence.* (2 Sam. 14:28)

The storyteller gives us some information about Absalom—he was extremely good-looking and a perfect specimen of masculinity. He had a magnificent head of thick hair that was cut only once a year. He was married, with three unnamed sons and a daughter he named after his sister, Tamar. Our ears perk up at this description— Saul was handsome, head and shoulders above everyone else, and his rulership ended in disaster. David was handsome and good-looking, attractive to both men and women, and the jury was still out on his leadership. Now we learn that Absalom was breathtaking—what are we to make of this?

In addition to being fine, Absalom was ambitious and smart. He was virile, fertile, and had a good family. David didn't want to see him but we certainly do. And like so many sons, Absalom wanted to see his father. It had been five years now and Absalom had had it. He tried to get Joab to help him. Absalom finally persuaded Joab to help him after he burned Joab's fields. And Absalom sent David an ultimatum through Joab. (Read 2 Sam. 14:32.)

David agreed then to see Absalom, who paid obeisance to his father, the ruler. David kissed Absalom. The scene is point blank and leaves lots of questions (see 2 Sam. 14:33).

- The language is formal—David was the ruler, and not father;
- Absalom bowed down before the ruler, not his father;
- Absalom behaved like a servant and not a son;
- The ruler kissed Absalom not like a father kissing his son.

This is an awkward scene and we can only speculate about what was happening here. Father and son had been separated for some five years. We expect there to have been rejoicing and celebrating. We hope for a heart-to-heart talk to air their differences. We wait for Absalom's plea for forgiveness and David's absolution. We are itching to hear words of welcome and reconciliation—what we get instead is a cryptic description of the father-son reunion. David yearned for Absalom the whole time he was gone. For two years, Absalom was just a call away and yet David never called for him. We don't know if David played with his grandchildren or if he had even seen them. We wait in vain for a joyous homecoming. What did Joab think as he observed the scene? What did Absalom think about his father's coldness? What did David think as he looked upon the heir apparent and successor to the throne? So many questions . . .

We are jarred back to reality in the very next verse:

After this Absalom got himself a chariot and horses, and fifty men to run ahead of him. (2 Sam. 15:1)

We must wonder what Absalom was up to—was his desire to see his father a real attempt at reconciliation? If his father had welcomed him with love and forgiveness, would Absalom have responded in kind? We will never know because Absalom was plotting his takeover. Absalom made a stunning move against David—more evidence that he *was* his father's son. He established a small army, highlighted the weakness of David's administration, and shamelessly charmed the people to his side. (Read 2 Sam. 15:3–6.)

Absalom was the paragon of patience and worked his planned takeover for four years. At that time, he asked permission from David to go to Hebron to worship God (remember that David was made ruler of Judah at Hebron). David granted him permission, when all the while Absalom was planning a coup. Surprisingly, David did not question Absalom's motives nor did he become suspicious of his sudden desire to worship at Hebron instead of Jerusalem. Absalom was calculating and ruthless—just like his father.

At Hebron, he declared himself ruler. Imagine that—he even had the support of Ahithophel, a member of David's administrative staff. Absalom worked undercover to usurp the throne. What happened? How did David let this happen? David seemed to be as clueless as Saul was. We expect more from David—he was the ideal ruler, but he as slipping, slipping, slipping—into what, we cannot say yet.

When David heard about Absalom's plot, he fled for his life. The mighty ruler comfortably enthroned in his capital city was once again a man on the run. David spoke in urgent tones—get up! Hurry! But there was time for his entourage to prepare for the journey. David took the time to inventory those leaving Jerusalem with him: his household (except for ten of his concubines left to watch the house), his officials, his laborers, and six hundred Gittites who followed him from Gath, including Ittai (see 2 Sam. 15:19–22). David and company moved en masse toward the wilderness. Even the priests Abiathar and Zadok marched out of the city, carrying the ark of God. David ordered them to return the ark to the city—David didn't seek God's guidance but rather expressed a weak hope that God would allow him to return to the city. It was not a given anymore, however, that God would grant David's wish.

David was clearly down but not yet out—he seemed alert as he handled business, deciding who left and who stayed behind. That he ordered certain folks to stay behind in Jerusalem—the concubines, Zadok, Abiathar, Ahimaaz, Jonathan, and the ark of God—indicates that he had not given up all hope of returning to his city and to his throne.

Still, he was a pitiful sight, trudging up the Mount of Olives, weeping and barefoot with covered head—supposedly overcome with grief. It is reasonable to believe David was being sincere in his grief; however, we give pause when he gets the news that Ahithophel has defected to Absalom's side. David, in the midst of his weeping and trudging, said a prayer for his former administrator. (Read 2 Sam. 15:31.)

Not only that, he enlisted the services of Hushai to trick Absalom and thereby gain valuable information. Hushai joined the espionage and the plot thickened. David developed a web of spies designed to thwart Absalom's plot to overthrow him and assume the throne.

David next encountered Ziba, into whose care Jonathan's disabled son Mephibosheth had been entrusted. David tried to gauge where his loyalty lay—Ziba didn't answer for himself but states that Mephibosheth was in Jerusalem hoping to regain the crown in his grandfather's name. Using royal prerogative, David transferred Mephibosheth's holdings to Ziba. It is not clear if Ziba was on David's side or simply using the opportunity to his own advantage.

The next episode on David's flight from Jerusalem is an interesting one—he encountered Shimei, a relative of Saul, who threw stones and curses at David. The man was quite nervy because the ruler's army surrounded him, but he didn't care. (Read 2 Sam. 16:7–8.)

It seems that staunch followers of Saul were hoping that Saul's house, through Mephibosheth, would be restored to the throne—

hope dies hard. Despite David's efforts to either eliminate or smooth over the tensions between Saul and himself, nothing worked. The followers of Saul were bitter and resented David and rejoiced in this turn of events. They held David responsible for Saul's death and saw Absalom's rebellion as just desserts for David.

David took Shimei's abuse in stride, but Joab's brother (and David's nephew) Abishai was livid. He and Joab had already taken care of Abner, so Shimei would be a nuisance easily snuffed out. But David was smart enough to know that killing Shimei would only undermine his efforts to regain the throne—there was no time to be wasted on the likes of Shimei. David had bigger fish to fry—namely his son Absalom, who now occupied Jerusalem, David's own city (see 2 Sam. 16:9–14).

As David and his company continued their flight, Shimei constantly pelted David with stones and insults. David neither confessed to nor denied the charges that Shimei leveled against him. David took the high road, relying on God's grace to vindicate him. David arrived at the edge of his territory, the Jordan River, where he refreshed himself—he had a long day ahead of him, if Absalom had anything to do with it.

The story continues with high drama, suspense, and almost unbearable intrigue—would Absalom pull off the coup and be crowned ruler? Would David come to his senses and handle his business? Would David's spies be able to get needed information to him? Would Joab and Abishai control their killing instincts? Will Shimei ever tire of hurling insults and stones at David? Would God intervene somehow? Let's see what happens.

Absalom and the Israelites now occupied Jerusalem. Absalom had to plot his next move. Hushai, David's friend and spy, played the espionage game quite well as he greeted Absalom:

> When Hushai the Archite, David's friend, came to
> Absalom, Hushai said to Absalom, "Long live the king!
> Long live the king!" (2 Sam. 16:16)

Absalom was suspicious because he knew that Hushai was a loyal follower of David. Hushai assured him that he had defected from David's camp to Absalom's. In fact, he was convinced that God had already anointed Absalom, and so he would follow God's man. Absalom believed him without further interrogation—this was way too easy. Either Absalom was not as bright as we thought or his ego was such that he wanted to believe that Hushai had been won over. Hushai was possibly using code language—he never identified the "ruler" nor the "one" God and the people had chosen. This might be a case where Absalom heard what he wanted to hear; certainly, he assumed he was the one of whom Hushai spoke.

Absalom consulted his council about how to get rid of David. His chief counsel was Ahithophel, who served as a seer-prophet. (Read 2 Sam. 16:23.)

Absalom was convinced of his loyalty and trusted his judgment. Ahithophel first advised Absalom to take David's concubines so that all Israel would know that he was usurping the throne. Absalom would gain the support of the masses and of those dissatisfied with David's leadership. It was a bold move and could backfire—but Absalom was ready to go the distance to claim the crown. Ahithophel's advice takes us back to Nathan's censure of David. (Read 2 Sam. 112:11-12.)

Nathan's words were coming to pass—David was a fugitive, and his son had taken over his city and was now about to take David's "wives" (or concubines) as a show of power over his father. Once Absalom did this, there would be no turning back; this was a major move that would either make him ruler or get him killed. Absalom was ready:

> So they pitched a tent for Absalom upon the roof; and
> Absalom went in to his father's concubines in the sight of
> all Israel. (2 Sam. 16:22)

Ahithophel proposed that he lead the charge to kill David—he knew that David was tired, weary, and distressed. It was the perfect time to strike—get him while he was down. It was a brilliant strategy. By doing this, Ahithophel guaranteed that he would bring all the people back to Jerusalem, the coup would be complete, and Absalom would be the man—the new man!

Absalom hesitated and asked Hushai what should be done— bad, bad, bad move, Absalom. Don't do it! But did Absalom listen to us? No! He listened as Hushai laid out his plan. He began by reminding Absalom that David was down but by no means out. David was a warrior—he was a warrior's warrior and his entire posse was composed of warriors. And what do warriors do? They fight! Even then, Hushai said, David was rising like the phoenix from the ashes, regrouping in order to retake what was rightfully his. On top of that, David was fit to be tied with anger over this turn of events.

"If you think he's going to rollover," Hushai continues, "you had better think again. When David strikes, it will be all over for you, buddy! Now here's what you need to do . . ." Hushai suggested that Absalom call in the troops from all over Israel and that he, Absalom, lead a charge against David. Absalom would slay David and his followers, and what a grand feat it would be—and Absalom would owe no one, for he would have done this all by himself.

Now, if you had to choose between these two options, which would you choose:

- PLAN A: simple, direct, easy—strike now and take out the ruler. No fuss, no mess—a clear execution with no collateral damage and only one funeral.

- PLAN B: send a memo and wait for the troops to pack their gear, say goodbye to their wives and children, make their way to Jerusalem to get their orders, leave Jerusalem, go into the wilderness, kill everyone and maybe die in the process, come back to Jerusalem, bury the multitude of the dead, then prepare for the coronation.

Okay—plan A or plan B? Remarkably, Absalom chooses plan B and we can see the disaster just up ahead. Of course, the storyteller lets us in on why Absalom chooses Hushai's plan. (Read 2 Sam. 17:14.)

Aha! So God was back and working things out—and there was no way Absalom would win this one. In the middle of the story, we already know who would win—the rest of the action was almost anticlimactic.

When Ahithophel learned that his plan had been trumped by Hushai, he saw no future for himself: Absalom would be dead and David would be unforgiving of his defection. There was no way out for him, and Ahithophel hanged himself (see 2 Sam. 17:23).

Absalom finally made his way to Gilead and prepared for the showdown with his father. David and his company continued to receive hospitality and support (see 2 Sam. 17:27-29). David divided his army into three groups—one commanded by Joab, one under Abishai, and the third under Ittai the Gittite (who was newly attached to David and thoroughly loyal—see 2 Sam. 15:19-22). David's army was massive compared to Absalom's, which had only one commander.

David's troops encouraged him to stay behind and let them take care of business. David reluctantly agreed and asked for only one thing. (Read 2 Sam. 18:5.)

Despite the desperation of the situation, David still loved his son and wanted him to emerge alive from this bloody mess. It seems that David, even in the midst of the biggest battle of his career, could not completely forget that his enemy was also his son. He commanded mercy for his son—and all the people heard David's plea. We don't know the commanders' or the people's reaction to David's request. With David's words ringing in their ears, the army went to meet Absalom. There was no contest—the battle belongs to David. (Read 2 Sam. 18:7-8.)

We know, of course, that Absalom didn't stand a ghost of a chance, and his army suffered massive casualties. And where was

Absalom? Had he avoided the massacre? Was he hiding in order to regroup and attack again?

Absalom was riding a mule through the forest and his hair got tangled in the branches of an oak tree. Before he could untangle himself, the mule kept going and Absalom was left hanging from the tree. What a pitiful sight he was—dangling by his magnificent locks, flailing and thrashing about. But there was no one to help him. This young, handsome upstart dangled between heaven and earth—helpless, vulnerable, and all alone.

If David's commanders dealt gently with him, Absalom would live to see his father again. And who knows—perhaps reconciliation could happen. A man saw Absalom dangling from the tree and informed Joab.

Joab, who risked his relationship with David to bring Absalom out of exile; Joab, whose heart went out when Absalom asked him to set up a meeting between his father and himself; Joab, who understood the depths of David's love for his rebellious son—rather than call for help for Absalom, Joab lashed out at the man reporting. (Read 2 Sam. 18:11.)

The reporter refused to lift a hand against the ruler's son—there was not enough money in the world to force his hand. He had heard David's plea and he was not about to defy the ruler. Joab couldn't believe his ears—he dismissed David's plea as mere sentimental dribble. (Read 2 Sam. 18:14-15).

Joab proved ruthless still—he just wanted the matter to be over. Joab made sure that Absalom was dead, really dead, really, really dead!

The rebellion was over and Joab . . . er, that is, David was victorious. Joab was in total command and stopped the fighting by sounding the trumpet. Absalom's troops scattered and fled into the woods. Absalom's body was disposed of and then David had to be updated. Joab sent a Cushite (Ethiopian) servant to tell David the news, but Ahimaaz insisted that he run with the news. As the two approached Mahanaim, David was sitting by the city gates waiting.

Ahimaaz arrived first with the war summary, "All is well." But David asked pointedly, "Is it well with the young man Absalom?" (2 Sam. 18:29). But Ahimaaz, the son of the priest Zadok, could not bear to tell the ruler that the young man was dead. Then the Cushite servant arrived with the good news that the coup had been defeated. Again David asked, "Is it well with the young man Absalom?" (2 Sam. 18:32). The servant relayed that Absalom was dead.

And David lost it—his hopes for gentle treatment had been dashed. His hopes of seeing his son alive were gone. David could only weep the cry of any parent who loses a child prematurely. (Read 2 Sam. 18:33.)

The young man who killed his half brother to avenge his sister's sexual violation had once again become "son." The young man who set up his half brother's execution had once again become "son." The young man who fled into exile for three years—once again "son." The young man who spent two years waiting for his father's hug and kiss—"son" again. The young man who forced his father out of his own city—now "son" again. The young man who lay with his own father's concubines—now "son" again. The young man for whom David pleaded gentleness—"son" once more.

David, who had been so eloquent when lamenting Saul and Jonathan and Abner, was reduced to one pitiful and anguished cry:

> *"O my son Absalom, my son, my son Absalom! Would*
> *I had died instead of you, O Absalom, my son, my son!"*
> *(2 Sam. 18:33b)*

David, the grieving father, could only weep and mourn. His family had been torn apart and he had just escaped the clutches of a son who would have killed him for the crown. David mourned all that was lost, gone, dead.

Joab, on the other hand, understood that there was work to be done in the here and now. Joab was impatient with David—whimpering over a headstrong, murderous, rebellious, and ruthless son—enough already! Joab soundly chastised David for neglecting his public duties; he was still the ruler and the territory had to be restored. What was more, David's grieving was an insult to the men who had risked their lives to save David's life and to save the territory. (Read 2 Sam. 19:6b–7.)

Joab stated the case forcibly and honestly; he gave David a dose of tough love. David had to shake off his grief and handle his business—long live the king.

David composed himself and took a seat at the city gate where the people were waiting. The Israelites who defected to Absalom were the first to recommit themselves to David. He pleaded with the people of Judah who sided with Absalom to rejoin the family. As a token of his sincerity, he appointed Amasa, Absalom's commander-in-chief, over his army.

This was not a good move. David desperately wanted to reunite the territory, but surely the death of Absalom did not eliminate the anti-David sentiments throughout the land. Absalom was charming and charismatic, but he would not have galvanized people if there had not been discontentment among the people already. David had learned a valuable lesson and had do whatever he could to appease the dissenting factions in his territory. He bargained with his kinfolk by offering a top cabinet job to his nephew, Amasa; David conveniently forgot that Amasa had lost the battle. Nonetheless, it was Amasa who persuaded the people of Judah to rejoin David.

As David made his way back to Jerusalem, those he saw on his earlier flight met him. Shimei, of the stones and curses fame, asked for forgiveness and claimed David as his ruler. Of course, Abishai still wanted to kill Shimei, but again David prevents it. David publicly renounced Abishai's impulsiveness and bloodthirsty ways (see 2 Sam. 19:22).

Mephibosheth, who had stayed in Jerusalem hoping to reclaim the crown for the house of Saul, came out of Jerusalem to meet David. David asked why he had stayed behind and Mephibosheth explained that his servant, Ziba, had deceived him and slandered him. Mephibosheth said he never had eyes for the crown. He accepted David as God's chosen. David had given Mephibosheth's property holdings to Ziba; rather than punish Ziba, David now divided the holdings between the two. As a show of loyalty, Mephibosheth didn't take his share.

Barzillai the Gileadite, who had provided food for David when he was in Mahanaim, met David at the Jordan River. David offered him a place in Jerusalem. He refused the offer but suggested that his son Chimham join David; and so he did.

There was a tug of war between Israel and Judah over who had the greater claim on David—a sign that the division between the north and the south was not over (see 2 Sam. 19:41–43). We will not be surprised, then, to learn that the territory split after Solomon's death.

There is one last episode to look at before we close this long chapter on King David. On the heels of Absalom's rebellion and defeat, another rebellion broke out. Sheba, a Benjaminite, refused to recognize David as the ruler. (Read 2 Sam. 20:1–2.)

When David returned to Jerusalem, he set his house in order by putting away his concubines left behind; they lived as widows because of Absalom's violation of them (see 2 Sam. 20:3).

David was clearly back in charge and wasted no time handling the Sheba situation. He ordered his new commander-in-chief, Amasa, to bring the troops of Judah to Jerusalem in three days for a strategy session. Amasa could not get the job done in the allotted time. This was a major faux pas on Amasa's part. We know that Joab would have had the troops in place in two days! But David had made his choice and would not admit he'd made a mistake by appointing the inept Amasa.

David ignored Amasa and laid out the situation to the blood-thirsty and politically incorrect Abishai. (Read 2 Sam. 20:6.)

As it so happened, Amasa bungled the job; he met the troops at a large stone at Gibeon where he ran smack dab into Joab! With one blow to the intestines, Joab effectively killed Amasa. With no remorse—war is death, death is death—Joab joined his brother

Abishai to go get Sheba. Amasa was blocking the road as he lay in his blood. (Read 2 Sam. 20:12–13.)

Amasa was a mere stumbling block and, once he was moved, the action continued. Neither Joab nor Abishai missed a step. Sheba hid out in Abel of Beth-maacah. The warrior brothers were willing to destroy the city to capture Sheba; but a wise woman struck a deal. She would make sure that Sheba's head was thrown over the city wall if Joab would spare the city. He agreed, and a woman saved the city.

Joab sounded the trumpet indicating that the fight was over. The troops returned home and Joab went to Jerusalem. Joab had reclaimed his office as commander-in-chief. He rejoined David's cabinet—the territory was back intact (see 2 Sam. 20:23–26). He and David never discussed Joab's demotion and they never discussed his rehiring. Things moved along as if nothing had happened.

As 2 Samuel winds to a close, we find David continuing his reign. We hope that after the Sheba rebellion was put down, David could enjoy the fruits of his labor and live to a ripe old age in peace. Such was not to be the case, however. We are alerted that the business with Saul was not yet over. (Read 2 Sam. 21:1.)

We remember that ancient peoples' fortunes and misfortunes hinged on the quality of their relationship with their god(s). For Israel, the nation prospered when ruler and people were obedient and faithful to God. Likewise, unfortunate events or circumstances were directly related to some breach in the covenant relationship on the nation's part. The immediate task, then, was to make up for the breach and to set things right again.

We are told that a three-year famine was God's judgment on Israel because Saul killed the Gibeonites, a group of non-Israelites promised asylum in Israel (2 Sam. 21:1–9). The Gibeonites were occupying the land when the Israelites arrived under the leadership of Joshua. The Gibeonites devised a clever plan to avoid extermination, and their plot worked. Joshua spared them and made them "hewers of wood and drawers of water" for the congregation and for the altar of YHWH (see Josh. 9:1–27).

After three years of famine, David's first act was to ask the Gibeonites what happened and what needed to be done to make things right. They said that Saul had tried to kill them off after Joshua had promised them a place in Israel. They didn't want money and they didn't want to kill for the sake of killing—but if David would give them seven sons of Saul, that would make things right. David willingly complied but did not turn over Jonathan's son, Mephibosheth, to honor his oath to Jonathan.

David handed over to the Gibeonites two of Saul's sons and five of his grandsons. The seven men were summarily executed at the beginning of the barley harvest in late spring. The Gibeonites left the bodies in the open where birds and wild animals could pick at the flesh. But Rizpah, grieving mother and stepgrandmother, kept watch over the bodies until the rains came, which signalled the end of the famine. She watched and protected the bodies for six months!

When David heard about her vigil, he had Saul and Jonathan's bones exhumed from Jabesh-gilead and held a mass burial for them and the seven slain in Benjaminite territory in Zela, where Saul's father, Kish, had a family tomb.

The rains came, the famine was over, and Gibeonites were satisfied. On the surface, David had acted in good faith—all was well in the land again. There were, however, some quite troubling elements of the story:

- Why did David wait three years before approaching God about the famine? Year after year, the famine ensued, but no one was seeking God's help.
- Why did God only speak to David about Saul's bloodguilt and why the judgment now, so long after Saul's death?
- Why was there no record of Saul's killing of the Gibeonites?
- Why did David have to convince the Gibeonites to seek expiation for Saul's bloodguilt? They sought the seven men only after David insisted they do something (see 2 Sam. 21:3–6).

These are puzzling questions that have some scholars believing that David's hands were dirty here. It was easy to use the famine as a means to get rid of possible threats to his throne by Saul's descendents. How convenient for David! We have seen that the followers of Saul continued to harbor hope that Saul's legacy would be restored in Israel—but with sons and grandsons gone, David would have no problem with the house of Saul. Obviously, Jonathan's lame son did not threaten David; and David could maintain his innocence since the Gibeonites effectively executed the last of Saul's immediate line. So, once again, we see David's ruthless side, yet he was able to maintain his innocence in a matter that worked to his advantage.

In this same episode, we see something else. As news of Rizpah's silent vigil, week after week, all day and all night, reached David, he was moved. We don't know what moved him—compassion or guilt—but he was smart enough to know that *he* now had to do something. Rizpah was Saul's concubine over whom Ishbaal and Abner separated. She appeared as a silent witness to the brutality of men and their power. They might kill but they were not absolved of guilt or judgment. Her silence and steady watching remind us that we must not ignore the casualties of power and might.

David arranged a mass funeral and burial for Saul, his sons, and his grandsons at the tomb of Saul's father. David did right by the house of Saul, right? Right!?

Before David died, he endured and guided all Israel through a famine, the final extinguishing of Saul's house, another series of wars with the Philistine, a census, and a plague. David moves through these trials and tribulations—not quite the strong warrior we've known. But God had promised David an everlasting dynasty—we see how fragile the territory was after an auspicious start under David's leadership.

David had been on an incredible journey from tending his father's sheep to keeping a grasp on a fractious territory. After the early glory days of war and politics, David sunk into the abyss prompted by his lustful desires. God did not abandon David but held him accountable for his actions. David paid the cost for committing adultery and murder by battling his own family.

David made some brilliant moves—he united the northern and southern tribes. We learn that not all was peaches and cream, but for a time, Israel was a strong nation—independent with an expanding empire. David surrounded himself with smart, competent men who were loyal to him and to the territory. He brought unity by establishing his capital city in neutral territory, Jerusalem. He built a palace and administrative buildings, signaling that Israel was, indeed, like the other nations. He appointed a cabinet of trusted leaders who understood his vision and commitment to making Israel a powerful state. David brought the ark of God to Jerusalem and appointed priests to oversee religious life. He centralized both the political and religious life in Jerusalem. His political creation had spiritual sanction—another brilliant move. He established a strong military base with his personal troops forming the core. David was practical, cold, calculating, creative, clever, and cunning. He set his course and moved steadfastly forward. David loved God and God loved him. God promised him an everlasting dynasty. David, good looking and handsome, had it all: power, money, status, and women.

Yet with all at his disposal, his lust for Bathsheba was his undoing. His violation of her, including the murder of her husband, set a course for familial bloodshed and death. David never confronted Joab about his secret killings. We don't know how much David knew about Joab's unofficial activities; but it is clear that David could not make it without him. The one time David tried, the experiment ended miserably; Amasa was simply no Joab.

David never completed his administrative agenda. He did not judge cases among the people and did nothing to ensure that justice was meted out equitably. David never disciplined his closest allies—they did whatever suited them, especially Joab and Abishai.

David's parenting skills were inadequate and he was not able to stop the family dysfunction that haunted him. Because we don't see much of David's inner thoughts or feelings, we cannot say why he didn't do something about his children. Perhaps he resigned himself to Nathan's prophecy; if God decided to judge him through his family, David may have felt helpless to resist his fate. Perhaps as a youngest son himself, he just didn't know what to do about his sons. He certainly didn't learn much about parenting from Saul. Saul's own children defied him in order to support David.

Despite his flaws, David is lifted up as the ideal ruler. The biblical storyteller is careful to make clear that David was the ruler sanctioned by the people and by God—with the hope that the rulership thing would turn out well this time.

David made a good start. He married politically important women who helped him form a strong international network of alliances. His capital was not just a political city, it also was the religious city. His leadership broke the old tribal patterns so that people owed allegiance to the state rather than to their tribes. We will see, however, that old ways die hard.

Whatever we may think about David, we cannot ignore him. We must either love him or hate him. There is very little middle ground with him. We are left feeling sorry for Saul who never got a fair chance to be ruler. Saul began his reign hiding among the luggage and ended his reign falling on his own sword. His loyal followers tried to keep his memory alive but to little avail.

David, more complex and less accessible, leaves us wondering. We want to know what made him tick; we want to know what fire burned in his belly; we want him to have been sincere, caring, and real. When he mourned for Absalom, we want to believe that he somehow mirrored our own reaction to the premature deaths of children.

We don't see David interacting much with his wives and children. So while we see the intimate details of his children's actions, we long to see the real David. We want him to be better than he was—but after getting our hopes up, in the end, he let us down, just as Saul did.

Yet we cannot let David go. He has a hold on us that we can't shake off. Perhaps the attraction we have for David is that he reminds us so much of ourselves. He was so thoroughly human with all the complexities that brings. And he loved God—when David is good, he's very good. When he's bad, he's horrid—and that is what we relate to in him. He was bewildering and puzzling, yet there was something in him that resonates with the ambiguities and layers within us all. Long live the king!

REFLECTION QUESTIONS

1. How do you evaluate David's overall leadership?

2. How does one balance personal and public life?

3. How did David deal with conflict? How do you deal with conflict? Are your methods working for you? Why or why not?

4. David had trouble communicating with others. What advice would you offer him about his communication skills?

5. How would you deal with David's situation with his children, especially Amnon, Tamar, and Absalom?

6. How did David understand power? How did he misuse his personal power? How did he use his public or royal power?

7. David was a warrior and an artist. How did he balance these very different aspects of his personality? Are you left brain or right brain? How do you balance the two?

8. Did David have trusted confidantes? Is it important to have persons whom you trust as part of your leadership team? Explain.

9. Consider your leadership style. Are you a team player or lone ranger? How effective are you as a leader?

10. In what ways do you practice self-care? Do you need to adjust your methods? Explain.

5 · SOLOMON

MAMA SAYS I DESERVE THIS!

Read 1 Kings 3:16–28, 6:11–14, 11:1–3

Solomon was David's son; his mother was Bathsheba. Solomon took the throne in the midst of controversy. Neither David nor his prophets clarified the process by which future rulers would be chosen. This lapse opened the way for all kinds of drama to ensue around who became ruler. And Solomon set the tone for violence and bloodshed associated with the top job in the nation.

David closed his reign with an important deed that would have consequences long after he died. In 2 Samuel 24, we are told that God was again angry with Israel but we don't know why. God ordered David to take a census of the territory. Without question or conversation, David ordered Joab and the commanders of the army to take the census. When Joab protested, we suspect something deeper was happening here. David overrode Joab's reluctance but did not give an explanation for the census. It took nine months and twenty days with the help of military presence to number the able-bodied men: eight hundred thousand in Israel and five hundred thousand in Judah.

When the census was done and reported, David was stricken and confessed his "sin" to God. It is not clear why taking the census ordered by God was a sin on David's part. God didn't correct David nor did God offer any explanation. We, too, are confused. David's prophet, this time Gad rather than Nathan, came to David with an awful proposition (see 2 Sam. 24:13).

David was dumbfounded and left the choice to God. Without further ado, God sent pestilence throughout the land, and seventy thousand people died. God kept the avenging angel from destroying Jerusalem and the angel stopped at the threshing floor of Araunah the Jebusite.

David again confessed his sin and took responsibility for what he had done. We still are unclear about the exact nature of his sin (see 2 Sam. 24:17).

Again, Gad brought a message to David from God. He was to build an altar on the threshing floor. David approached Araunah, who wanted to give his property, including animals for sacrifice, to the ruler. David did not accept the gift but insisted on paying Araunah a fair price. David built the altar and the pestilence ended.

This puzzling episode raises more questions than it provides answers for:

- We are confused by the actions of God in this event—why was God angry with Israel? Why did God order David to count the people and then act as though the divine hand was not involved? Why did God offer David, through the prophet, three undesirable options to rectify the sin? Why did God not take responsibility for God's anger and let David off the hook?

- We are confused by the actions of David in this event—why did David not question God's command? Why didn't he ask God to help him understand what was happening? Why was David unable to choose from among the three choices? Why didn't David share with Joab that the census request was God's doing? Why did David ask that he alone be punished only after seventy thousand had already died?

The lessons from the narrative are not as satisfactory as we want. God appears to have been a tyrant who killed innocent people. Let us remember that when bad things happen, the people automatically blamed themselves. In this case, the census coincided with a plague in the land. Perhaps the two were connected and David, as ruler and leader, did what he could to reconnect with God by asking for divine mercy.

At the end, God extended mercy and stopped the devastation. Whether in good times or bad, God was sovereign and ruled with compassion. And David remained the one who prayed, confessed, and repented. From his indecisive moment to his request that God punish him and not the people, we see a leader who cared about his people and who trusted God to hear his prayer. We see a David who, despite all the royal power and privilege he enjoyed, still worshiped the God who is faithful, merciful, and compassionate. The narrative ends as it began—with prayer and worship.

The journey from Hannah's barrenness to the closing days of David's reign has been a bumpy, bloody, and bewildering one. We have gone from the loose federation of tribes to a strong unified nation with all the stresses and tensions that change brings. We've seen a parade of personalities march across the landscape—Hannah, Eli, Samuel, Saul, Jonathan, Michal, David, Abigail, Nathan, Bathsheba, Joab, Abner, Ishbaal, Mephibosheth, Absalom, Tamar, Rizpah, and others who exercised power. Through their stories, we learn that ultimate power belongs to God. When we next see David, we are amazed—he is old, frail, bedridden, and sexually impotent. (Read 1 Kgs 1:1–4.)

David's oldest living son, Adonijah, in consultation with commander-in-chief Joab and priest Abiathar, assumed he would be the next ruler. Although there was no policy about royal succession, it was presumed that the oldest son would inherit the crown. There was a hint that Adonijah's coronation would bring problems—the priest Zadok, Benaiah, Nathan, Shimei, Rei, and David's own warriors did not side with Adonijah.

While Adonijah was planning his coronation, Nathan and Bathsheba were plotting to make Solomon the next ruler. Nathan initiated a conversation with her that smacks of conspiracy:

> *Then Nathan said to Bathsheba, Solomon's mother, "Have you not heard that Adonijah son of Haggith has become king and our lord David does not know it? (1 Kgs 1:11)*

Nathan coached Bathsheba on what to say to David, who would have some say in who succeeded him. Nathan assured her that he would eavesdrop on her talk with David and come in to verify her words.

Bathsheba's audience with the ruler was filled with intrigue—David was described as "very old"; his new young and beautiful concubine, Abishag, was with him but there was no indication in the text that Bathsheba even acknowledged her presence. Bathsheba, silent in her first encounter with David, was now verbal and in charge—she gave him an earful, invoking guilt and highlighting his decline and possible memory loss (read 1 Kgs 1:17-21).

As she ended her speech, Nathan arrived. After paying obeisance to the ruler, he repeated Bathsheba's speech and added that Adonijah had not included key people at his celebratory party (see 1 Kgs 1:26)—including Nathan, Zadok, Benaiah, and Solomon. David sent for Bathsheba again and promised the throne to Solomon (read 1 Kgs 1:29–30).

He confirmed his promise by calling in Zadok, Benaiah, and Nathan; David declared Solomon ruler and instructed the men to take Solomon to Gihon, where he was to be anointed the ruler of

Israel. Solomon was to ride David's own mule as a symbol of his leadership. Solomon was to sit on David's throne with David's blessing and consent. All went according to plan. (Read 1 Kgs 1:39–40.)

This turn of events piques our interest for several reasons:

- It makes us reconsider our assessment of Bathsheba. In 2 Samuel 11, she was silent except for her terse message to David, "I am pregnant" (2 Sam. 11:5). She appeared to be a victim of royal privilege, power, and prerogative. Here, however, she was in control. She paid obeisance to the ruler even as she ignored Abishag—as if her status as concubine required no acknowledgment from Bathsheba the wife. Although Bathsheba parroted the words Nathan gives her, she improvised and played her part superbly. It may be surmised that Bathsheba was no shrinking violet but rather a clever, savvy woman. Scholars are divided on how to evaluate her. Some maintain she was a helpless victim who was used and abused by a lustful ruler. Others say she was a calculating woman who worked a plan to make sure she had a son who would be ruler. Her actions certainly lend some credibility to the theory of Bathsheba as an active participant in the narrative and in her life.

- We also see Nathan in a new light. In 2 Samuel 11, he was the voice of reason and righteousness. He creatively constructed a parable that drew upon David's compassion and sense of justice. Nathan dared to convict David—"You are the man!" (2 Sam. 12:7). Of course, we can attribute Nathan's daring to his obedience to God's command. Here, however, it is not clear what was motivating him. He used religious language, but we are not told that God actually chose Solomon. This seems to be something that Nathan initiated and Bathsheba bought into the possible deception.

- We have to see how David has declined. His sexual vigor was tied to his political vigor—that he was frail and weary and incapacitated is a mirror reflection of his lack of leadership fitness. Nathan and Bathsheba took the opportunity to manipulate David to do their bidding. The younger David would not have stood for such treatment. But this bedridden David could only give in and acquiesce to the direction of others. We are not sure if David ever promised the throne to Solomon—if he did, did he forget to tell anyone else or had he just not gotten around to it yet? If he did not promise the throne to Solomon, then the prophet and David's wife lied to achieve their desired end—Solomon on the throne.

While Solomon was anointed with grand fare in Gihon, Adonijah was feasting in En-rogel, thinking himself the ruler. Adonijah, handsome and obedient, was about to have a rude awakening. Joab heard the trumpet that signaled Solomon's rulership and wondered out loud about what the trumpet meant. At that moment, Jonathan, son of Abiathar the priest, arrived with devastating news for Adonijah. (Read 1 Kgs 1:43–46.)

Adonijah's party came to an abrupt end—smile and the whole world smiles with you; have the crown snatched away and you are left alone. Even Adonijah recognized that this cruel turn of events could be fatal. He went directly to grab the horns of the altar, hoping to find protection there from Solomon's wrath and sword. Solomon's response to Adonijah's plea for his life was cryptic—and we suspect that Solomon had something sinister up his sleeve. (Read 1 Kgs 1:52–53.)

King Solomon's first act was to send his brother home. Solomon spent some time with his dying father, who offered a charge for Solomon's leadership:

- Be strong and courageous;
- Follow God's ways and keep God's statutes, commandments, ordinances, and testimonies according to the law of Moses;
- Take care of Joab, whose hands are full of blood;

- Be kind to the sons of Barzillai;
- Take care of Shimei, who cursed and pelted David with stones; he has to go.

Solomon received his charge and took center stage when David died. His ascension to the crown was a marked changed from the early days of the monarchy when God chose the ruler by speaking to a prophet, who then anointed and blessed God's choice. We are left wondering why Solomon was the choice. He had not demonstrated any of the charismatic gifts of previous rulers. We don't know if he had military skills. We don't have a resume outlining his qualifications for the job.

Now the sitting ruler proclaimed the incoming ruler and outlined the details of the coronation. The question of who succeeded, though, still had not been determined. Solomon was not the oldest living son, but he was the designated ruler.

In the meantime, Adonijah sought an audience with Bathsheba, who was cautious but consented when assured that Adonijah came in peace. He was candid with her about the events. (Read 1 Kgs 2:15–18.)

He acknowledged that Solomon was the rightful ruler and asked Bathsheba to intercede with Solomon on his behalf—but his request was bizarre! He asked for one of the king's concubines, Abishag, for his wife. Remember that taking a ruler's wife or concubine was a bid to usurp the throne. But he may have thought the rule didn't apply since Abishag was still a virgin. But the question remains—why did he want her of all the women in the territory? And why did he ask Bathsheba to help him? He must have known that she knew the implications of such a request. Bathsheba surely did, and that was what she wanted; she agreed to talk to Solomon.

When she approached her son, he paid great respect to her and offered her a seat on his right side. She relayed Adonijah's request and, as we might expect, Solomon went ballistic. (Read 1 Kgs 2:22–25.)

Now just what did Adonijah think would happen? Solomon wasted no time filling his father's shoes. He immediately had his brother executed by Benaiah. He banished the priest Abiathar, who supported Adonijah's bid for the throne, to his hometown of Anathoth. Next in line for execution was Joab.

Brave warrior that he had been, Joab understood the seriousness of supporting Adonijah over Solomon and ran to the altar. He grabbed the horns of the altar. The altar served as a buffer between the condemned and the executioner. No one was to be killed while holding the horns of the altar. But Solomon ignored this prohibition and ordered Benaiah to kill Joab on the altar (1 Kgs 2:31–11).

Finally, Solomon placed Shimei on house arrest in Jerusalem. He was to stay in the city and not venture out under penalty of death. However, at the end of three years, Shimei went to Gath to recover two of his runaway slaves. When Solomon heard about Shimei's trip, he ordered Benaiah to execute him (see 1 Kgs 2:39–46). Solomon used this innocent infraction as an excuse to kill Shimei.

Through a series of executions, Solomon thus took care of traitors and rebels. David's hands were cleansed of the blood of those executed with and without his knowledge. Solomon took care of the loose ends of David's reign—the territory was free of bloodguilt, oaths had been kept, and the future of David's house was secure. Solomon clearly saw himself as a man on a mission; even the execution of Joab at the altar was justifiable. Solomon was taking to heart his father's charge. (Read 1 Kgs 2:2–4.)

Solomon began his reign with a clean slate. Through murders and strong-arm tactics, Solomon secured the throne—long live the king!

Solomon's reign occurred during a time of relative peace. There were no major wars for Israel at the outset. Since Solomon had taken care of any political threat to his territory, he could turn to other duties and projects. He appointed Benaiah as commander-in-chief and Zadok as priest. Solomon married Pharaoh's daughter and struck an alliance with the Egyptians. This was the first indication that Solomon's reign would be an international one. In this, Solomon followed David's pattern of politically beneficial marriages.

We are given a hint that the religious life of the ruler and the people might become an issue. (Read 1 Kgs 3:2–4.)

Idolaters also worshiped at the high places. It was curious that Solomon worshiped at Gibeon when the ark of God, the symbol of God's presence, was in Jerusalem. During a time of sacrifice, God visited Solomon in a dream. Solomon dreamed a conversation between God and himself. God asked Solomon what he wanted. In a speech clearly shaped by D, Solomon responded: as God had shown great and steadfast love to David; as David was God's servant; as David walked before God in faithfulness, righteousness, and uprightness of heart; as God had granted David a son to sit on the throne—Solomon was humbled that God had chosen him to be a servant ruler, even though he was a "little child" (with this term, Solomon was denoting humility; who am I to lead your people?) to rule over God's chosen people who were so numerous they couldn't be counted. Solomon's request was eloquent:

> *Give your servant therefore an understanding mind to*
> *govern your people, able to discern between good and evil;*
> *for who can govern this your great people?"* (1 Kgs 3:9)

His prayer was sincere and reflects God's high hopes for Israelite rulership. While the other nations had rulers who focused on wealth and power, Solomon asked for wisdom. While other rulers sought security through might, Solomon asked for a heart to serve. While other rulers sought human honor, Solomon asked for the strength to walk in God's ways. Solomon seemed to have his priorities in order. God would grant what Solomon asked and those things that he hadn't asked for—long life, honor, riches, protection from enemies, a discerning mind, and a loving heart. In other words, Solomon would have it all—as long as he walked in God's ways and kept God's statutes and commandments. We wonder if Solomon was able to walk the walk and talk the talk. We are already on edge because Solomon worshiped in the high places.

When Solomon awoke from his dream, he was immediately put to the test by two mothers, who happened to be prostitutes and needed to determine to whom a surviving son belonged—read 1 Kgs 3:16-27. Solomon's proposed solution to cut the living child in half was enough for the one of the mothers to speak up on behalf of the child.

As Solomon considered the case, he demonstrated his capacity to listen with his heart and to discern what was right. He did not ask questions of the women. He, in his wisdom, judged the case without testimony from the mothers. If Solomon was willing to judge a case between two prostitutes, he would surely judge all cases fairly. The case involved birth, death, deception, and puzzle—Solomon did not jump to conclusions but considered how best to uncover the truth. We don't know who the real mother was at the end. We know that the first woman was more fit to have the child. The point of the story seems not to determine the biological mother but rather to indicate that God's wisdom was invested in Solomon. Solomon could be trusted to administer justice to the powerful as well as the powerless, to men as well as women. Solomon had exercised great wisdom in the matter:

> *All Israel heard of the judgment that the ruler had rendered; and they stood in awe of the ruler, because they perceived that the wisdom of God was in him, to execute justice.* (1 Kgs 3:28)

Both Saul and David were preoccupied with fighting wars—internally among the tribes and externally with surrounding nations. As a result, neither was able to set up a governmental structure from which to govern. Because Solomon did not have major battles to wage, he was able to organize his territory, and he was a good organizer and administrator. He developed quite a bureaucracy that included holdovers from David's reign as well as newcomers on the scene—see 1 Kgs 4:1–6. The most startling change Solomon made was in the division of the territory.

Until his reign, the territory had been divided according to the twelve tribes. But Solomon established districts that did not coincide with the tribes. He placed a chief administrator over each district. The twelve administrative districts formed two circles that represented the extent of the expanded territory plus one official over Judah (read 1 Kgs 4:7–19). Included in the list were two of Solomon's sons-in-law: Ben-abinadab, married to Taphath, and Ahimaaz, married to Basemath. Other appointees had either a family or friendship connection to Solomon. Solomon was taking care of his family and friends, a hint that there might be trouble ahead.

In addition to restructuring the territory away from tribal connections, Solomon imposed a tax schedule. Each district was responsible for one month's provision for the ruler and his household:

> *Solomon had twelve officials over all Israel, who provided*
> *food for the ruler and his household; each one had to make*
> *provision for one month in the year. (1 Kgs 4:7)*

There is no mention of funds or provisions for God. Apparently Solomon's court had taken on a life of its own. The storyteller conveys that Solomon's territory was wide and vast. Each district and other holdings paid tribute (taxes) to the ruler for the upkeep of the palace and the royal court, and the people were happy to do so:

> *Those officials supplied provisions for King Solomon and*
> *for all who came to King Solomon's table, each one in his*
> *month; they let nothing be lacking. (1 Kgs 4:27)*

In other words, things were great in Israel and all the people were safe and happy. One gets the impression that peace and prosperity were the order of the day. However, there are some subtle hints that all was not well in the territory. Solomon extended the *corvée* or cadre of forced labor. These were persons required to serve in various capacities in the territory. The *corvée* started with David as he built his palace and other administrative building projects. The building projects multiplied under Solomon and required manual labor as well as foodstuffs and provisions for the ruler's army. Solomon probably thought that things would run smoother if the people were not tied to the old tribal lines of loyalties. He created something that would be easier to control and maintain. In addition, the new configuration embraced and included new territories that were now part of the overall territory. We are taken back to Samuel's warning about what rulership would mean. (Read 1 Sam. 8:11–18.)

Furthermore, the new districts seemed to grow out of the census that David conducted and for which he repented. Things are beginning to become clearer. The biblical storyteller gushes with compliments about Solomon. (Read 1 Kgs 4:29–30, 34.)

Solomon was the man, for sure! He stood head and shoulders over others; the land had never seen one like Solomon; he was known far and wide as the wisest, the most artistic, the most knowledgeable ruler there had ever been—and all were gifts from God. Solomon was a blessed man, indeed.

Solomon's burning desire was to build a suitable house for God. Remember that David wanted to build a temple but was prevented by God through a message from the prophet Nathan. Solomon seemed to have the go-ahead to begin construction. Solomon struck a deal with King Hiram of Tyre, a deal that put Solomon in debt year after year (read 1 Kgs 5:10–11). In addition to incurring high debt, Solomon required massive numbers of laborers—both Israelites and outsiders. (Read 1 Kgs 5:13–16.)

The temple that Solomon built was magnificently exquisite. While we cannot reconstruct the Temple in our imagination, we get the sense of the structure—it was massive in scale, plenty spacious enough to accommodate the people for worship; there were plenty of breakout rooms or side chambers; the edifice was multistoried; there were winding stair cases; it was made of the finest wood and stone; the building had intricately carved panels with lots of gold inlays; there were carved cherubim, palm trees, flowers, and pomegranates throughout; it contained bronze pillars, stands, baths, basins, pots, and shovels. This was a tremendous building project and only the finest materials were used. The construction of the Temple is detailed in 1 Kgs 6–7. In the middle of the description we find a reminder that the house being built was for God. (Read 1 Kgs 6:11–13.)

The statement may also be a warning that it was not the building that would ensure God's presence but the hearts and minds of the ruler and the people. If they followed God's ways, then God would dwell among them. We wonder how this will play out since Solomon had invited foreign powers to join the construction effort. And Solomon was forcing people to build—taking them away from their homes and lives for three to four months at a time. He was also extracting taxes to support the royal court while the construction went on. Seems like a formula for disaster.

At the same time that the Temple was under construction, Solomon had other projects going on to complete the royal campus: the House of the Forest of Lebanon (1 Kgs 7:2), most likely the treasury building and armory; the Hall of Pillars (1 Kgs 7:6); the Hall of the Throne (1 Kgs 7:7); the Hall of Justice (1 Kgs 7:7b); Solomon's personal residence (1 Kgs 7:8); and a fabulous home for his wife, Pharaoh's daughter (1 Kgs 7:8b).

We are duly impressed with Solomon's building program. He enlisted the services of Hiram of Tyre (not the ruler; this was a different Hiram), an artisan whose specialty was bronze work. A special chamber was built to house the ark of God known as the Holy of Holies. (Read 1 Kgs 6:19–20.)

We are not to lose sight that this house was God's—even though the most visible sign of God's presence would sufficiently be hidden in the innermost chamber of the Temple. We are informed that the Temple was built in seven years, but Solomon's own house took thirteen years to complete. Moreover, as impressive as the Temple was, it was not the biggest building in the royal complex— the House of the Forest of Lebanon was larger than the Temple.

When the Temple was complete, Solomon brought in David's things—silver, gold, and various vessels—to be stored there. The building now housed the old and the new.

Once all the construction was complete, Solomon called a grand celebration to dedicate the Temple and to transfer the ark of God to its permanent resting place, the Holy of Holies (see 1 Kgs 8:1–12). All the people gathered in Jerusalem around the time of the Feast of Tabernacles (also known as the Feast of Booths)—a festival of thanksgiving and a ritual of renewal of covenant commitments held at the autumn harvest (see Deut. 31:9–13). Solomon's poem to God is poignant:

> *Then Solomon said, "[YHWH] has said that [God]*
> *would dwell in thick darkness.*
> *I have built you an exalted house, a place for you to dwell*
> *in forever." (1 Kgs 8:12–13)*

It highlights that God has promised to be with, or tabernacle with, God's people. And now a suitable house had been constructed so God might be with the people. However, the Temple was not the only place where God was—God was free to come and go. The house was the visible manifestation that represented one way that God tabernacled with the people. Solomon gve a long speech and prayer as part of the dedication ceremony. In this way, he was as articulate and eloquent as his father, David. Some things to note about Solomon's speech are:

- Solomon was grateful to God for fulfilling promises to David that his son would build a suitable house for the "name of YHWH," which was an indication that the Temple was symbolic of God's presence, which could not be contained (1 Kgs 8:14–21).
- Solomon petitioned that God honor the divine promise of an everlasting dynasty for David's house as long as David's descendants walked in God's ways (1 Kgs 8:25–26).

- Solomon petitioned for protection, safety, and harmony with neighbors (8:31), with Israel's enemies (8:33), with nature (8:35, 37), and with foreigners (8:41)—so that all people, inside and outside of Israel, would know and respect God's name. The petition contained seven situations for which God's presence was sought, to signify holistic coverage and concerns. This litany also outlined how Israel might avoid perilous situations—by turning to God. God was asked to "hear in heaven, and act, and judge [God's] servants, forgive" and to bestow God's mercy, compassion, and justice accordingly (1 Kgs 8:30–53).

- Solomon reminded the people of God's blessings. He said that the people could continue counting on God's presence and blessings as long as they were faithful and obedient to God by keeping the covenant commitments (1 Kgs 8:54–61).

Solomon closed the dedication with sacrificial offerings—animal sacrifices, burnt offerings, grain offerings—a fitting end to a fine ceremony. Solomon, then, dismissed the gathering. (Read 1 Kgs 8:66.)

The territory was large and unified; God had a suitable house; life was good; the people were happy; all was right with the world— all because of Solomon's leadership—long live the king!

This eighth chapter of 1 Kings is a summary of the D tradition and its theological perspective. Israel was the people of God chosen out of Egyptian bondage by God's gracious compassion to be a special people. Although Israel spent a time wandering in the wilderness, God was never absent from them; God provided for their needs and watched over them. God promised Israel a land where they were to be a light to the other nations. Through revelations to Moses, God provided instructions on how Israel was to be obedient and faithful to God only. When the people strayed from God, bad things would happen. If the people repented and turned back to God, God would hear them, forgive them, and act on their behalf. As long as the ruler and people walked in the ways of God as outlined by Moses, all wouldl go well for them. If they failed, they could expect God's judgment, which might take many forms—famine, drought, blight, plague, oppression from enemies, and even capture by other nations. The dedication of the Temple was an opportunity to rehearse the history of Israel's relationship with its God. The focus was that Israel was not just a political entity; it was also a spiritual entity that had as its source and sustainer the One God, YHWH, who committed to them eternally. Because of Solomon's faithfulness, Israel was at rest from war and was prosperous—God willed *shalom* (peace and well-being) for the nation and its people.

After all the pomp, circumstance, and celebration at the Temple dedication, God appeared a second time to Solomon. This time, God responded to Solomon's dedicatory prayer: God acknowledged Solomon's fine words; God offered Solomon an eternal dynasty over Israel as long as he walked before God with integrity of heart and uprightness. If Solomon or his children, however, failed to keep covenantal obligations by serving or worshiping other gods, then Israel could expect to suffer the consequences and repercussions of their actions. Israel would be removed from the land and the Temple would be destroyed. Israel would become the object of ridicule and pity and all would know that God had destroyed the nation. (Read 1 Kgs 9:9.)

Solomon was thus warned and he seemed to understand what was at stake. For obedient faithfulness, Israel would be blessed with peace and prosperity. Any deviation from God's plan would result in exile and ridicule. Sounds simple, doesn't it?

We are introduced to the Queen of Sheba in 1 Kings 10. Although we don't know where Sheba was located, legend has it that she was from Ethiopia and her name was Makeda. The queen had heard of Solomon's fame. What was it that she had heard? While we cannot know for certain, we can make some guesses:

- Perhaps she had heard about the twenty cities in Galilee Solomon gave to King Hiram of Tyre. This was the same ruler who supplied quality lumber and gold for the building of the Temple. Hiram was displeased with the cities Solomon offered, especially since Hiram also gave Solomon a large amount of gold (1 Kgs 9:11–14). It is clear that Solomon mortgaged off Israelite territory to bankroll his massive building projects.

- Perhaps she had heard about the *corvée* that provided a steady supply of laborers to work on Solomon's projects. In addition to the royal complex in Jerusalem, Solomon rebuilt Gezer, fortified a number of cities, established storage facilities throughout the land, constructed armories to house his chariots, and other projects (1 Kgs 9:15–19).

- Perhaps she had heard how Solomon forced the Amorites, the Hittites, the Perizzites, the Hivites, and the Jebusites into slave labor (1 Kgs 9:20–21).

- Perhaps she had heard how Solomon appointed Israelites to be soldiers, officials, commanders, and captains for his armed forces (1 Kgs 9:22).

- Perhaps she had heard how Solomon offered sacrifices and offerings of well-being three times a year on the altar he built to God (1 Kgs 9:25).

- Perhaps she had heard about Solomon's fleet of ships on the coast of the Sea of Reeds, or the Red Sea (1 Kgs 9:26–28).

Surely, what she had heard included some scope of Solomon's wheelings and dealings, international trade and diplomacy, public and religious duties, and business and administrative savvy. Solomon was known the world over as a smart, pious, wise man whose true worth and wealth were unknown. Solomon's administrative abilities were renowned and he was said to preside over a happy, prosperous state.

So the Queen of Sheba journeyed to Jerusalem to see what the fuss was about and to pose some "hard questions" to the wonder ruler.

We don't know the nature of her questions, but we surmise that she sought to match wits with Solomon. He was a willing partner and further dazzled her with his abundant hospitality. (Read 1 Kgs 10:4–5.)

After she caught her breath, she gave voice to what the narrator wants us to understand about Solomon: that his wisdom and prosperity were due solely to God's grace. (Read 1 Kgs 10:9.)

She left Solomon with gifts of gold, spices, and precious stones. She was no inferior looking for a handout; she was, in every way, his equal—she was wise, business savvy, and wealthy. He reciprocated with gifts for her.

Other symbols of Solomon's glory included large amounts of gold from traders, merchants, rulers, and governors from throughout the land; a great ivory throne overlaid with gold; drinking utensils of gold; a fleet of ships that brought more gold as well as silver, ivory, and exotic animals. Other rulers sent abundant gifts to Solomon— he was the man, for sure—long live the king! (Read 1 Kgs 10:23–25.)

Things were going so well for Solomon, it's nearly impossible to see how things could have gotten any better. He was revered and respected all over the world. He had the world on a string and life was so good! Solomon was a ruler like those of other nations—only better. He had stockpiled minerals, precious stones, splendid weapons, and fancy accessories. Israel's experiment with rulership seemed to be working at long last. Right? Well . . . maybe . . .

In the midst of all of Solomon's accolades and accomplishments, we read something that makes us pause. (Read 1 Kgs 11:1–4.)

Oh-oh! Trouble was brewing here! Not only did Solomon love forbidden women, he also worshiped their gods and goddesses. And the ominous note gave way to utter disaster:

> *So Solomon did what was evil in the sight of [YHWH],*
> *and did not completely follow [YHWH], as his father*
> *David had done. (1 Kgs 11:6)*

If that isn't enough, Solomon built altars for the gods of his foreign wives (see 1 Kgs 11:7–8). Well, well, well—the perfect ruler had a flaw, after all. We don't expect this from Solomon—"Solomon loved [YHWH], walking in the statutes of his father David; only, he sacrificed and offered incense at the high places" (1 Kgs 3:3). Solomon had two visions where God strictly outlined the conditions for the well-being of his dynasty—see 1 Kgs 3:1–15 and 9:1–19.

Solomon had a staggering number of women in his life—seven hundred princesses and three hundred concubines. The reference to princesses indicates that most of his marriages were politically motivated. We have seen how such liaisons lead to alliances with other nations and can be quite advantageous to national security; David also took on wives for political reasons. However, his wives did not sway David from God. David was able to maintain his faith in God and was not tempted to worship the gods of his wives.

Solomon apparently lacked David's steadfastness. We are reminded that Solomon worshiped God at the high places even though the ark of God was in Jerusalem; perhaps, old habits die hard. At any rate, Solomon violated Deuteronomic law that strictly forbade the worship of foreign gods. (Read Deut. 17:2–7.)

In addition, Solomon overstepped the bounds of leadership also outlined in Deuteronomy. (Read Deut. 17:14–17.)

Solomon's good times were about to come to an end. What promised to be an incredible period of peace and prosperity was sinking into an abyss of sin and consequences.

How did Solomon allow this to happen? Was he so full of himself that he began to believe his own press? Is it that the tendency had always been there and that was why God visited Solomon, not once, but twice to impress upon him the requirements for peace and prosperity? God was angry, and Solomon's reign would come to an end. (Read 1 Kgs 11:9–11.)

Once again, the sin of the parent would be visited upon the child. The territory of Solomon would be ripped from him as it was from Saul. Solomon's love for foreign women was not enough to violate the covenant obligation. But his willingness to indulge his wives' desire to worship their gods and his investment of time and labor to build altars to them were the last straws. Enough already, God seemed to say. Since Solomon was so open to other gods and other styles of worship, let him go ahead and indulge. In the meantime, God was working behind the scenes to rip the territory from Solomon.

Rather than move directly into the next phase of Solomon's reign, we are next taken "backstage" to see what had been happening while Solomon was falling into idolatry. God was raising enemies against him—two outsiders and one insider.

The first outside threat was Hadad the Edomite. The story of Hadad went back to the days of David and Joab. Edom was a site of victory for David, who overtook it and killed some eighteen thousand of its citizens (see 2 Sam. 8:13–14). Hadad, in line to succeed his father, was taken to Egypt. In Egypt, Hadad found favor with Pharaoh; married Pharaoh's sister-in-law and became part of the royal family; and had a son who was raised in Pharaoh's court. When Hadad learned that David and Joab were dead, he asked Pharaoh to let him return to his own country. We cannot miss the similarities between Hadad's story and the story of Moses (see Exod. 2:1–10). Although Hadad was not part of Israel, God would use him to bring about God's will for Solomon and his royal house. And we wonder if this will connect to the storyteller's reminder that Solomon also married a daughter of Pharaoh (1 Kgs 7:8; 9:16, 24).

The second outside threat was Rezon. He fought against King Hadadezer of Zobah, who was defeated by David and nearly destroyed (see 2 Sam. 8:3–6 and 10:15–19). Rezon escaped the persecution, became leader of a group of bandits (similar to David's posse), captured Damascus, and set up his own Aramean territory. Again God, who controlled everything, used another international leader to muck up Solomon's reign.

We have been led to believe that Solomon's reign personified peace and harmony. Now we learn that both Hadad and Rezon had given Solomon problems:

[Rezon] was an adversary of Israel all the days of Solomon, making trouble as Hadad did; he despised Israel and reigned over Aram. (1 Kgs 11:25)

Solomon's inside threat was Jeroboam, whose father was an Ephraimite. Jeroboam was a servant of Solomon's. Jeroboam had an encounter with Ahijah, a prophet from Shiloh (where Eli was priest—the person who had mentored Samuel). Although Jeroboam was young, Solomon saw great potential in him. Solomon was so impressed that he elevated Jeroboam to supervisor over all the forced labor of Joseph's house. The prophet Ahijah tore his new garment into twelve pieces. (Read 1 Kgs 11:31–32.)

The reason Solomon was losing the territory was because he had forsaken God and worshiped foreign gods. Ahijah said that God would not take the whole territory. In order to honor God's promise to David, God had Solomon rule over one tribe, Judah, and Jeroboam would rule over the ten northern tribes. Jeroboam was given a promise like that given to David and Solomon. (Read 1 Kgs 11:37–38.)

God's eternal promise continued to carry conditions. And the standard was set for the rest of the monarchy. If rulers kept God's statutes and commandments and followed the ways of David, all would go well and they would be judged positively. If they failed, they would be judged wicked and have the territory taken away.

There are several parallels to note here. First, Saul tore the hem of Samuel's garment, which symbolized his loss of the territory. (Read 1 Sam. 15:27–28.) A similar action by Ahijah denotes how God would rip the territory from Solomon (1 Kgs 11:30).

Second, David was a young man who found favor in the eyes of King Saul. Saul was so impressed that he elevated David to be his armor bearer (1 Sam. 16:21). Solomon did the same with Jeroboam.

Third, when Saul realized that David was chosen by God to succeed him, Saul tried to kill David. And Solomon tried to use the same tactic to protect his crown:

Solomon sought therefore to kill Jeroboam; but Jeroboam promptly fled to Egypt, to King Shishak of Egypt, and remained in Egypt until the death of Solomon.
(1 Kgs 11:40)

It will be interesting to see what happens when Solomon dies. So, what can we say about Solomon's leadership? His ascension to the throne was unusual. He did not take an active role in claiming the throne. He seemed content to let Adonijah take the crown because we don't know Solomon's reaction. It was Nathan who worked on his behalf. Nathan devised a plot to install Solomon and enlisted the help of Solomon's mother, Bathsheba, to convince the infirmed and impotent David to name Solomon as his successor. Once crowned, however, Solomon wasted no time eliminating every threat to his crown, including killing his brother, killing his father's enemies, and banishing minor threats from Jerusalem. Because we hear of no major battles, we can only assume that Solomon may have had some military intelligence.

His genius lay in his administrative abilities and skills. He established a royal bureaucracy that set up a conscripted labor force as well as a taxation schedule. He did not eliminate foreigners but rather exploited them as his labor force.

Solomon oversaw a massive construction project that included the Temple, a couple of palace houses, and other administrative buildings. He installed military bases at strategic points throughout the territory. He purchased a fleet of ships that broadened his trading enterprises. He appointed his family and friends to key administrative positions and engendered trust and loyalty from leaders near and far.

He was secure enough to spend quality time and to match wits with the Queen of Sheba. He was wise and pious—he loved God and received God's blessings. His weakness seemed to be women—seven hundred wives and three hundred concubines. He allowed his relationships to take his focus off God, and that was the cause of his downfall.

Solomon, however, represented a total break with the old ways of Samuel and Saul. Solomon even restructured the nation—moving away from tribal divisions to districts. But as we shall see, the old tribal loyalties did not die. Even God's sanction against Solomon resorted back to the tribes.

Now we know that Solomon's son, Rehoboam, had to deal with the repercussions of his father's sin. Israel's experiment with rulership continued to flounder!

REFLECTION QUESTIONS

1. Describe Solomon's leadership style.
2. What were Solomon's leadership strengths? What were his weaknesses?
3. Solomon asked God for wisdom. Did he use this gift well? Explain.
4. Was Solomon a "mama's boy?" Did his relationship with his mother affect his leadership? Explain.
5. Have you ever had oversight for a building or renovation project? What leadership challenges does this kind of project present?
6. How do you understand social and economic class distinctions? What are the implications of class for leadership?
7. What do we learn about Solomon in his interaction with the Queen of Sheba? Explain.
8. How does a wise man like Solomon still manage to anger God? In what ways does God anger you? How do you deal with your anger?
9. What would David say to Solomon about parenting skills?
10. In what ways are you like Solomon? Explain.

PART TWO

THE DIVIDED TERRITORY
Israel and Judah

What is it about power that makes people lose their minds? The fight for the throne is a story of blood and gore with no clear winner. This fight began a downward spiral that eventually resulted in the fall of both Israel and Judah.

We've come to a decisive turning point in Israel's history. When we started our journey, we watched a loose federation of twelve tribes struggle to work and live together as people of the God, YHWH. They were never quite able to overcome their family jealousies and disputes. The threat from outside forces, especially the Philistines, forced them into a tenuous alliance for the sake of their survival. The old pattern of the judges gave way to national leadership embodied in Samuel—judge, prophet, priest. While Samuel was a good leader, he left no suitable heirs to assume his leadership role. Israel began an experiment with rulership and acclaimed Saul as its first ruler. Saul, while an able warrior, had personality and mental health issues. His volatile temper, paranoia, and impatience with process made him an undesirable ruler.

David was a rising star who dazzled all who came within his orbit. His early years as a protégé of Saul, his wilderness days as a renegade warrior, and his contrite heart catapulted him to the monarchy, where he ruled supreme. If not for his indiscretion with Bathsheba and subsequent murder of her husband, David's record would have been nearly perfect. He was able to rationalize the violence and blood that characterized his reign. God also thought his leadership was effective.

David's son Solomon made a good start as ruler but fell way short of the standard set by his father. Solomon loved women from other countries and soon found himself promoting the worship of the gods of his wives. For the D storyteller, this was the great taboo and meant that the evaluation of Solomon's rulership was a negative despite the glory he brought to himself and to Israel. Solomon would not lose his territory but his son would lose the territory.

So it is with great anticipation that we wait to see how God would bring judgment on Solomon's house. We wait to see if God would keep the divine promise to David for an everlasting dynasty. All bets were in jeopardy now:

> *Solomon slept with his ancestors and was buried in the city of his father David; and his son Rehoboam succeeded him.* (1 Kgs 11:43)

We don't know if Rehoboam, Solomon's son, knew that the territory would be ripped from him because of his father's sin. We know that he was ready to take on the crown. He traveled to Shechem, a city in the hill country of Ephraim. Shechem held historical importance for Israel: it was the first city Abram (Abraham) visited on his journey from Haran (see Gen. 12:6–7); and it was the site where Joshua gathered all the people to present themselves before God (see Josh. 24:1ff). The city was also an important place for the northern tribes. All of Israel was in Shechem to anoint Rehoboam the next ruler.

Jeroboam, who was in exile in Egypt because of Solomon's contract on his life, hearing about the pending coronation of Rehoboam, returned to Israel. He joined the assembly as they make a request of the ruler-elect. (Read 1 Kgs 12:3b–4.)

The people of the north complained about Solomon's forced labor and heavy taxes. They sought relief from their burdens under Rehoboam. If he agreed to a compromise, the northern tribes would pledge their allegiance to him. Rehoboam asked for three days to consider their request, which the people granted.

Rehoboam ignored the advice of the elders who encouraged him to accept a compromise. If Rehoboam had exercised common sense, he might have been able to delay or even stop God's judgment that doomed the united territory. By compromising today, Rehoboam might gain the support of the Israelites forever. Rehoboam, however, seemed not to like their advice. He consulted his peers; they are called "young men" but were in their early forties. His contemporaries advised him to strut his royal power and show the people who the man was! Not only was he not to lighten their load, he was to enforce the load with whips. (Read 1 Kgs 12:10–11.)

They encouraged him to insult the people and guarantee more severe burdens. The Hebrew translated "my little finger" in 1 Kings 12:10 may actually mean "my penis," which was a sign of macho bravado and was quite insulting.

Rehoboam did not listen to the people. This was an action opposite of what his father did. Common sense should have dictated that he take the advice of the elders, but the storyteller reminds us that Rehoboam's response was part of God's plan to take the territory from him—see 1 Kgs 12:15.

Israel did not back down from its position—they were bigger and stronger and were weary of being ruled by those insensitive boors from the south. Rehoboam had forced their hands, and the Israelites living in the north withdrew from the territory. (Read 1 Kgs 12:16.)

Rehoboam, now ruler over only the Israelites living in Judean towns, flexed his royal muscle by sending Adoram, the supervisor of forced labor, to force the rebellious Israelites to rejoin the territory. What was Rehoboam thinking? If the deciding issue was the burden of forced labor, why would you send the supervisor of forced labor to talk to the people?? The Israelites stoned Adoram to death! As a sign of his own courage and swagger:

> *Ruler Rehoboam then hurriedly mounted his chariot to flee to Jerusalem. (1 Kgs 12:18b)*

The text continues and is a bit confusing. In verses 3 and 12 of 1 Kings 12, Jeroboam was part of the assembly that requested and heard the answer to their request for a change in labor and tax policies. Yet in verse 20, it's as if Jeroboam had just returned from Egypt. Scholars have not yet resolved the difference. The end result was that Jeroboam was made ruler over Israel. The territory was now divided:

- Israel consisted of the ten northern tribes, whose ruler was Jeroboam;
- Judah consisted of the tribe of Judah at Jerusalem, whose ruler was Rehoboam.

When Rehoboam arrived back at Jerusalem, he assembled the house of Judah and the tribe of Benjamin to mobilize against Israel in an effort to restore the territory. He had some 180,000 troops at the ready; but he was advised by the prophet Shemaiah to let the matter go. Rehoboam could not and would not win this fight—because it was God's doing:

> *"Thus says [YHWH], You shall not go up or fight against your kindred the people of Israel. Let everyone go home,*

for this thing is from me." So they heeded the word of
[YHWH] and went home again, according to the word of
[YHWH]. (1 Kgs 12:24)

It is not clear where the tribe of Benjamin landed in the controversy. It didn't go with Israel but had not pledged allegiance to Judah.
However, since Benjamin was right at the border of Jerusalem, it was
important that Judah maintain close relationship with Benjamin.

The action will now speed up as we watch the succession of
rulers in the separate territories. The D storyteller will weave the
stories of the rulers, moving back and forth between the two territories. To the Bible reader, the stories may seem confusing—the time-
line is difficult to follow; keeping the names of the rulers and their
contemporaries straight will be challenging; dates, events, and even
names overlap and contradict each other. Some of the stories are
longer than others; some have stories within stories. Some of the
stories are only a couple of verses long. The storyteller ultimately
conveys the idea that although we are dealing with two territories,
there is only one story—the rise and fall of Israel.

What we know is that Israel, the northern territory, would fall
in 722/721 B.C.E. Judah, the southern territory, would fall in
587/586 B.C.E. Each story of the monarchs follows a pattern that
includes an evaluation of the ruler's leadership. The criteria for evaluation are how closely the ruler followed God's statutes and commandments and how well he walked in the ways of David. As we
will see, most northern rulers receive negative evaluations while
most southern rulers are judged more positively. In the list of monarchs, there is one woman, Athaliah, the daughter of Ahab and
Jezebel, who ruled over Judah.

We will not be able to study all the monarchs in Israel's history.
I have chosen in part 1 to take detailed looks at the leadership of
Saul, David, and Solomon.

The following charts show all the rulers in the divided territories of Israel in the north and Judah in the south. We will examine

DIVIDED TERRITORY: Israel

Monarch	Length of Reign	Relationship to to Predecessor	Leadership Assessment
JEROBOAM	22 years	Adversary	Negative
NADAB	2 years	Son of Jeroboam	Negative
BAASHA	24 years	Adversary	Negative
ELAH	2 years	Son of Baasha	Negative
ZIMRI	7 days	Adversary	Negative
TIBNI	?	Adversary	?
OMRI	12 years	Adversary	Negative
AHAB	22 years	Son of Omri	Negative
AHAZIAH	2 years	Son of Ahab	Negative
JEHORAM/JORAM	12 years	Brother of Ahaziah	Negative
JEHU	28 years	Adversary	Negative
JEHOAHAZ	17 years	Son of Jehu	Negative
JOASH/JEHOASH	16 years	Son of Jehoahaz	Negative
JEROBOAM II	41 years	Son of Joash/Jehoash	Negative
ZECHARIAH	6 months	Son of Jeroboam II	Negative
SHALLUM	1 month	Adversary	Negative
MENAHEM	10 years	Adversary	Negative
PEKAHIAH	2 years	Son of Menahem	Negative
PEKAH	20 years	Adversary	Negative
HOSHEA	9 years	Adversary	Negative

DIVIDED TERRITORY: Judah

Monarch	Length of Reign	Relationship to Predecessor	Leadership Assessment
REHOBOAM	17 years	Son of Solomon	Negative
ABIJAH/ABIJAM	3 years	Son of Rehoboam	Negative
ASA	41 years	Son of Abijam	Positive
JEHOSHAPHAT	25 years	Son of Asa	Positive
JEHORAM	8 years	Son of Jehoshaphat	Negative
AHAZIAH	1 year	Son of Jehoram	Negative
ATHALIAH	6 years	Mother of Ahaziah of Judah	Negative
JOASH/JEHOASH	40 years	Grandson of Athaliah	Positive
AMAZIAH	29 years	Son of Joash of Judah	Positive
AZARIAH/UZZIAH	52 years	Son of Amaziah	Positive
JOTHAM	16 years	Son of Azariah/Uzziah	Positive
AHAZ	16 years	Son of Jotham	Positive
HEZEKIAH	29 years	Son of Ahaz	Positive
MANASSEH	55 years	Son of Hezekiah	Positive
AMON	2 years	Son of Manasseh	Negative
JOSIAH	31 years	Son of Amon	Positive
JEHOAHAZ	3 months	Son of Josiah	Negative
JEHOIAKIM	11 years	Brother of Jehoahaz	Negative
JEHOIACHIN	3 months	Son of Jehoiakim	Negative
ZEDEKIAH	11 years	Uncle of Jehoiachin; younger brother of Jehoahaz	Negative

some in more depth than others. In particular, we will look at Rehoboam and Jeroboam, who presided over the division of the territory. We will close with looks at Hoshea and Zedekiah because they were in office when their respective territories fell. In the middle, we will look at Athaliah as the only queen in the group. The others will be mentioned but not studied in depth.

For a treatment of Ahab, please see my previous works: "Jezebel: Devious or Diva?" in *Bad Girls of the Bible: Exploring Women of Questionable Virtue* (Cleveland: Pilgrim Press, 1999), 53–64; and "Ahab and Jezebel: The Same Difference," in *Krazy Kinfolk: Exploring Dysfunctional Families of the Bible* (Cleveland: Pilgrim Press, 2005), 68–77.

6 · Judah—REHOBOAM

I'M THE MAN, FOR REAL!

Read 1 Kings 14:21–31

Now that we understand how Israel became a divided state, we begin our parade through the histories of Israel and Judah as separate nations. Judah was the smaller of the two territories and fairly isolated geographically. There was relative stability in the succession of rulers because of God's promise to David. We expect there to be tensions, however, between those who were connected to the royal court and the overwhelming majority of people who lived in the rural areas and worked for a living as farmers and shepherds. So we see the beginnings of class stratification in the territory between the haves and the have-nots.

Since most of the people were working class, they probably held to more traditional religious expressions. The cosmopolitan air of Jerusalem with its international flair was sure to be a source of discontent among the "common folks."

The last time we saw Rehoboam, he was fleeing Shechem and the wrath of the northern tribes. His refusal to lift the burdens of forced labor and taxation resulted in the north seceding from the union. Rehoboam was forced to return south to rule over Jerusalem, Judah, and those Israelites (northerners) in southern territories.

The D storyteller gives a terse account of Rehoboam's reign. We expect good things from him—he was the son of Israel's wisest and most successful ruler. But his diplomacy skills left much to desire. His arrogant, macho style alienated the northerners, and Rehoboam did nothing to smooth over their differences. We are alerted by the storyteller that whatever hopes we have for a good outcome for Rehoboam, well, we can just forget it.

Rehoboam ruled over Jerusalem, which was not just any city; it was not even just any capital city. Rather, Jerusalem was the very city where God had chosen to put God's name—of all the tribes and cities, it was Jerusalem where God's name presided and resided. After being hit over the head with this fact, we are dismayed to read the next line—Rehoboam's own mother was an Ammonite. Naamah was one of Solomon's wives and he permitted his wives and concubines to continue worshiping their native gods. Not only that, he built for them shrines and altars and other religious structures. Remember that all evidence of other gods was to be utterly destroyed as Israel settled into Canaan. (Read Deut. 7:1–5.)

For allowing the flourishing of foreign gods in the nation, we expect dire consequences. The D storyteller makes it quite clear to us. (Read 1 Kgs 14:22–24.)

We can only sit by to see what devastation was to be visited upon Jerusalem and Judah. Pharaoh Shishak of Egypt invaded Jerusalem and raided the Temple. He took the fine golden shields Solomon had made. Rehoboam paid a high price to Shishak. The Egyptian left Jerusalem and Judah weakened but not destroyed.

Rehoboam replaced the golden shields with bronze shields. The Egyptian leader violated Jerusalem and the Temple but neither structure was destroyed; nor was any judgment raised against Rehoboam or his house. Compare this with the harsh condemnation of Jeroboam in the north.

Rehoboam was spared, as was Jerusalem because it was the place where God resided. But there was no rest in the land for him. Rehoboam constantly battled Jeroboam. As the book closes on Rehoboam, we are reminded again of his ancestry:

> *His mother's name was Naamah the Ammonite. His son Abijam succeeded him. (1 Kgs 14:31b)*

So what can we say about Rehoboam's leadership? He had a difficult job of maintaining some sense of stability and order as he helplessly watched Israel separate and become two rival states. The split surely had devastating consequences for Judah, the smaller of the two territories.

With Israel gone and many of its territories declaring their independence, Rehoboam must have presided over a financial disaster—no labor, no taxes, and no tributes coming into the treasury. Rehoboam's own arrogance and insensitivity did nothing to put his reign on more solid ground.

In his interactions with others, he was foolish, crass, tactless, mean, nasty, oppressive, lacking wisdom, and unyielding. As the child of an international, multicultural union, Rehoboam permitted a wide range of tolerance in the territory, and no doubt idolatry was difficult to contain in such a free atmosphere. How was he going to tell his mama that she had to give up her gods?

Solomon had already instituted a policy that integrated Canaanite populations more thoroughly into the territory. It would now be difficult to think about cleansing the land—although this did happen later in the story.

We see that Rehoboam lacked diplomatic skills and basically had no class!

REFLECTION QUESTIONS

1. What were Rehoboam's leadership strengths and weaknesses?

2. Was there any way Rehoboam could have prevented the division of the territory? Explain.

3. How does one save face after making a big leadership mistake?

4. How important is it to compromise in leadership situations? What advice would you offer Rehoboam about his leadership style?

5. What advice would you offer Rehoboam about his conflict management skills?

6. Rehoboam gave in to peer pressure. Is this a challenge for you? If so, in what ways and what are you doing about it? If not, how do you avoid falling into the trap?

7. Have you ever made leadership decisions based on your ego needs rather than the needs of the company or organization? What was the outcome? Would do you anything differently if you had the chance?

8. What advice would you offer Rehoboam about managing the massive leadership challenges he faced?

9 What advice about leadership might David have offered Rehoboam? What leadership advice might Solomon have offered?

10. Are you part of a leadership team? What are the advantages and disadvantages of teamwork?

7 · Israel—JEROBOAM

ACTUALLY, I'M THE MAN, FOR REAL!

Read 1 Kgs 12:25–27, 1 Kgs 14:15–16

Jeroboam became the first ruler of the new political entity, Israel. He assumed the rulership after the northern tribes left the unified territory following Solomon's death. Jeroboam had the task of creating a state from nothing. When Jeroboam assumed leadership, there was no capital city, no administrative structure, no military organization, and no official religion. There were some things that played to his advantage, though. The northern section of the old monarchy was larger and had more money. They also had more troops than the south. They had also incorporated more of the Canaanite population than the south. The job for Jeroboam was to get things in order. We presume that he was smart enough and had gifts for the work ahead of him. We learn nothing of his administration in the Bible. He most likely used Solomon's model; we don't hear of any widespread discontent, so we assume he modified Solomon's administration concerning forced labor and taxes.

The ten tribes would have remained in the union if Rehoboam, Solomon's successor, had considered their request for adjustments in the forced labor and tax policies he inherited from Solomon. But Rehoboam, influenced by his power drunk peers, had disregarded and disrespected his subjects to the north. Fed up with unfair practices and annoyed with governmental interference in their lives, the northern tribes seceded from the union and formed their own territory. They appointed Jeroboam as their first ruler. Jeroboam's rise to power had major parallels to that of David's:

- Both were designated rulers-elect through an oracle by a prophet; both would inherit territories "torn" from their predecessors;
- Neither ruler-elect was directly related to the ruler in office;
- Both were exiled for political reasons—to escape the wrath of the ruler;
- Both were acclaimed by the people as their rightful ruler;
- Both received a promise of eternal dynasties;
- Both were charged to keep God's statutes and commandments.

In fact, Jeroboam was encouraged to model his leadership after David's example; if he did, his house would reign forever. Because of these similarities to David, we have high hopes for Jeroboam. We hope that he would become the one to save Israel. We are optimistic; even though the territory was divided, there was a chance that God would reverse the divine judgment and the nation would be united again.

We must remember that the relationship between the north and south was never a solid one. Internal squabbles never ceased and David did a lot of finagling to hold the territory together. External threats helped David's attempt at unity; the absence of such threats as the Philistines gave people time to focus on the life they lived under the Judahite leadership of Solomon. Solomon's ambitious building program required labor and money and the northern tribes resented the government's interference in their lives. The fierce independence of the tribes never died. Solomon used the military to support and enforce his policies.

With a regime change, the northern tribes saw an opportunity to have Solomon's repressive policies modified. Rehoboam was too foolish to recognize the opportunity to strengthen his territory. He made a fatal mistake that split the nation. Of course, we are informed that all of this was God's doing because of Solomon's sin. So, it didn't really matter how Rehoboam reacted, the territory was not to be his.

Jeroboam took center stage as the first ruler of the new territory, Israel. He established his residence and capital at Shechem. You will recall that Shechem was the site where Joshua gathered all the people to renew their covenant commitment to God (see Josh. 24:1, 19–26). The city was centrally located and probably generated a minimum of tribal jealousy as the selected capital city. Jeroboam also rebuilt Penuel, the site where Jacob wrestled all night until he received a blessing (see Gen. 32:24–31; for a study of this episode in Jacob's life, see "Jacob: All That Heaven Allows: Part 2," in my *Bad Boys of the Bible: Exploring Men of Questionable Virtue* [Cleveland: Pilgrim Press, 2002], 56–73).

As in the case of Saul, we are able to eavesdrop on Jeroboam's inner thoughts:

> *Then Jeroboam said to himself, "Now the territory may well revert to the house of David. If this people continues to go up to offer sacrifices in the house of [YHWH] at Jerusalem, the heart of this people will turn again to their master, King Rehoboam of Judah; they will kill me and return to King Rehoboam of Judah." (1 Kgs 12:26–27)*

Although God had promised the territory, Jeroboam gave in to his insecurities and doubts. And this was the beginning of the end for him. Instead of placing his trust in God, he relied on his own power.

He took counsel, we presume, from those who made up his cabinet, although none were named. Jeroboam's next steps were horrendous and we are shocked by his actions.

First, he made two golden calves and presented them as gods for the people to worship. He placed one calf in Bethel and the other at Dan, two former regional centers of worship (for Bethel, see Gen. 28:18–19, 31:13, Judg. 21:2–4; for Dan, see Judg. 18:27–31). Apparently, Jeroboam chose cities with previous religious significance. He may have thought his choices continued a religious tradition known to the people before the monarchy; he did not think he was creating a new religion. Instead, he was offering the people more convenient alternatives at the edges of the new territory. By placing the calves at the religious sites, Jeroboam may simply have meant to say that God's presence was available at Bethel and Dan. It was probably that the calves symbolized God's presence in the same way that the ark of God did in Jerusalem.

There was an old tradition in Israel of using the bull as a pedestal or throne for the invisible God. In line with this was an ancient title for God, "the Mighty One of Jacob," where the word "mighty" means strength, might, or an animal of strength, or bull. Thus, the title for God is rightly read "the Bull of Jacob" (see Ps. 132:2, 5; Isa. 49:26, 60:16). The image of the bull symbolized God's power and strength rather than being a rendering of the divine image. It was, however, a small step from honoring the metaphor to actually worshipping the image. Such worship was strictly prohibited by the D tradition:

> You shall not make for yourself an idol, whether in the form
> of anything that is in heaven above, or that is on the earth
> beneath, or that is in the water under the earth. (Exod. 20:4)

The golden calves were a reminder of the people's idolatry during the Exodus. While Moses was convening with God, the people grew fearful and impatient. They asked Aaron to make gods for them to follow. Aaron collected their gold and made golden calves and declared them to be the people's gods—see Exod. 32:1–7 and Deut. 9:8–21. Notice that Jeroboam actually quoted the Exod. 32:4b passage. (Read Exod. 32:4 and 1 Kgs 12:28.)

The second error that Jeroboam made was in setting up two alternative worship sites. This was in violation of the command found in Deuteronomy 12:5–7 that called for a centralized place of worship. Since God had chosen Jerusalem as the place for the divine name, Jerusalem was the only legitimate site for worship.

To make matters even worse, Jeroboam set up altars on high places and anyone who wanted to be a priest was appointed! The law clearly designated Levites as priests. (Read Deut. 12:19 and Deut. 18:1–8.)

Jeroboam probably didn't trust the Levitical priests to be loyal to his administration. By naming his own priests, he was assured spiritual support for his political positions. While many governments used religious teachings to undergird their work, the prophets blasted governments for such moves. The point was that the priesthood's first loyalty was to God and not to the ruler. Rulers were under the same law as the people and had no special rights, privileges, or prerogatives.

The final error that Jeroboam made was creating an alternative festival; he appointed a festival for the fifteenth day of the eighth month to rival the Feast of Booths in Judah (see Lev. 23:33–36). It is likely that Jeroboam was making an adjustment that better fit the reality of the northern territory. Festival dates were set according to the harvest patterns of the south, which meant that the north was always a bit off. By changing the time of the festival, Jeroboam made celebration and sacrifice more convenient for his constituents. Also, he saved his people the stress of making pilgrimage to Jerusalem just when they needed to begin their harvest.

On the surface, Jeroboam did not create anything new—he made adjustments that kept the people of Israel in Israel. His concern about people defecting back to old ways was addressed by the conveniences he supplied. But to D, Jeroboam was leading the people into idolatry. He was held responsible for setting the stage for idolatry to occur whether it actually happened during his reign or not. As the first ruler of Israel, he set the pattern by which all future rulers would be judged. And, plainly and simply, he messed up.

His political moves to secure his territory led to serious religious and spiritual errors. As we learn later, the people did, indeed, lapse into idolatry and the priesthood became corrupt advocates for the status quo by doing the ruler's bidding. As we read 1 Kings 12:28–33, against the backdrop of D's theological framework, all we can say is, "No! No! No!" But Jeroboam could not hear us and we realize he was doomed.

The drama continues: an unnamed man of God visited Jeroboam as he was offering incense at the altar in Bethel. The man spoke to the altar itself and declared that there was another ruler coming, Josiah, who would burn the false priests on the same altar. (Read 1 Kgs 13:1–2.)

What an indictment; it was considered a desecration to burn humans on an altar—but Josiah, who wouldn't appear for some three hundred years, would do just that. As a confirmation sign, the unnamed man prophesied that the very altar by which he stood would be torn down and ashes poured out from it. King Jeroboam no doubt thought the man was crazy and deluded. Jeroboam stretched out his hand, maybe pointing at the man so his servants could grab him. But Jeroboam's hand withered—right before his very eyes. He could not draw his hand back to himself. At that moment, the altar was torn down and ashes poured from it.

Jeroboam then realized the man was a prophet and asked him to pray so God would restore his hand. The man of God did and Jeroboam's hand was restored. Once restored, Jeroboam invited the man to dine with him and he offered the man gifts. Jeroboam, who had been embarrassed and dishonored by the stranger, tried to regain his honor. By extending sincere hospitality to the man,

Jeroboam would show his generosity and willingness to invite his enemy into his home. The man, however, refused with stern words. (Read 1 Kgs 13:8–9.)

Another slap in the face for Jeroboam. The man did not retrace his steps when he left; he went another way. There may be some subtle symbolism here—the man came in one way, the wrong way, and left a different way—showing Jeroboam that his way was the wrong way. Jeroboam's way would lead to idolatry rather than faithfulness to the one true God. Perhaps he still had a chance to turn around, away from the current direction in which he was moving. Jeroboam's way was leading the people away from God but he must turn, change directions, if the people were going to be saved. But Jeroboam just didn't get it.

The man of God, who refused Jeroboam's dinner invitation, was tricked into eating with an old prophet in Bethel. The man was later killed on the road by a lion. The lion did not eat the man or the donkey he rode—a sure sign that his death was God's work (see 1 Kgs 13:11–32). Disobedience led to his demise and seemed to be the lesson of the story.

Jeroboam did not change, repent, or turn from his ways. By disobeying God's word, Jeroboam rendered null and void God's promise for an everlasting dynasty. He messed up, big time! We just wait to see how his reign would end. We don't wait for long . . .

Jeroboam's son, Abijah, fell ill. Jeroboam encouraged his wife to disguise herself and seek advice from the prophet Ahijah, who was at Shiloh. She disguised herself, packed gifts, and went to Shiloh. As soon as he heard her footsteps, Ahijah knew it was the queen. He had been warned by God of her arrival and about her concern for her son. Ahijah had bad news for the queen: although Jeroboam could have had it all, he had failed to follow in the footsteps of David. His failure would have devastating consequences. Because Jeroboam committed grievous sins against God, there was no hope for him or his house.

Instead of an everlasting dynasty, all males in Jeroboam's family would be cut off and destroyed. Those of Jeroboam's house who died would be eaten by dogs and birds (remember Rizpah's silent vigil over Saul's sons and grandsons in 2 Sam. 21:10). When the queen returned home, Abijah would die but all Israel would mourn for him. He alone would have a decent burial. God had already chosen a replacement for Jeroboam. God had given up on Israel and the territory would be crushed and the people exiled from the land—because Jeroboam had sinned and was causing the people to sin.

Ahijah's prophecies came to pass. There were some questions, though; not all of Jeroboam's sons were cut off because his son, Nadab, succeeded him. Surprisingly, Jeroboam was fired from his job (like Saul) but continued working for twenty-two years (see 1 Kgs 14:20).

So what can we say about Jeroboam's leadership? Well, he certainly let an opportunity slip through his fingers. He was not a bad person; he just made ill-advised choices. In fact, he didn't seek the prophet's advice until it was already too late. He seemed to care about his people and tried to make life convenient for them; of course, he was politically motivated in this. But this didn't make him so very different from other men in the Bible.

Jeroboam was impulsive, political, and headstrong. He was not above using religious symbols for his own political advantage. He became the poster child for evil and wicked rulers in Israel. But he really didn't have much choice—he had to do something to make his territory distinctive from the former monarchy. And the people had to have some sense of spiritual support for their action. Many of his constituents felt compelled to go to Jerusalem to worship. It would not do to have a political entity where people went back to the former state to serve God. His solution actually made sense. But not to those who shaped the tradition.

He used his wife for his own ends—her pitiful disguise reminds us of Saul and his desperate attempt to save himself at Endor (1 Sam. 28:8–19). Again, he was not the first to use his wife—remember Abraham and Jacob? But Jeroboam's actions led to total instability in Israel—they just couldn't seem to keep a ruler. There was mayhem, murder, and mutiny—it was all a big mess.

But the real culprit seems to have been God! God is depicted here as a mean, rigid, unforgiving deity who delighted in death and destruction. God's rules were so rigid that any infraction resulted in irredeemable doom. God did not seem to take into account one's intention—only actions mattered. This God demanded unconditional, unerring obedience. God used political events for divine ends and overreacted while expressing anger—even using coarse language.

At the same time, this brutish God expressed unexplainable mercy for the sick child and permitted a fitting funeral and burial for him. Thus, God's use of grace and judgment was unpredictable.

Jeroboam recognized the need for the northern tribes to create an identity separate from that of the united monarchy, but his tactics were wrong. Jeroboam never apologized for his actions nor did he repent of his sin. He set into motion a horrible chain of events—but there was no turning back to the old ways. The rulership thing did not get strengthened in the northern territory of Israel.

REFLECTION QUESTIONS

1 What were Jeroboam's leadership strengths? What were his leadership weaknesses?

2. What did Jeroboam learn administratively from Saul, David, and Solomon?

3. Have you ever been part of a start-up business, new church start, or another new venture? What are the challenges of such work?

4. What role does vision play in leadership? What do you think Jeroboam's vision was? Did he have adequate support for his vision? Explain.

5. What do you do when you know you have made a leadership mistake?

6. What advice would you offer Jeroboam about financial responsibility and management?

7. What role did the prophet play in Jeroboam's leadership choices?

8. What stresses you out about leadership? What do you do to take care of yourself?

9. What kind of leadership team should Jeroboam have had in order to succeed in his work?

10. How did Jeroboam deal with difficult people? How do you deal with difficult people?

8 · Judah—ATHALIAH

THE BEST MAN FOR THE JOB IS A WOMAN!

Read 2 Kings 11:1–21; 2 Chronicles 22:2–12

In the midst of stories about men and their use (and misuse) of power, we find this story of Athaliah. She was the daughter of Ahab and Jezebel and a staunch supporter of the cult of Baal. How she came to rule over Judah is quite an interesting story; she was the only queen who assumed the crown.

Athaliah came from a long line of leaders. Her grandfather Omri's fame lasted for generations after his reign, and there were numerous references to him in sources beyond the Bible. Omri was an excellent administrator and visionary leader. Under his leadership, Israel flourished, expanded its borders, and enjoyed brisk international trade. He was astute in arranging politically motivated marriages that led to strong military and trade alliances. The marriage of

Ahab and Jezebel was a prime example, although Ahab was judged by the D tradition the most wicked of the evil rulers because of his marriage to Jezebel.

Jezebel was a zealous believer in Baal and more than held her own ground and power against YHWH's prophet, Elijah. Jezebel was smart, was politically savvy, and knew how to get what she wanted. She was both tender and merciless; pious and cold blooded; loving and treacherous. She was a layered and complex personality—but the D storyteller had absolutely nothing good to say about her. She was blamed for establishing Baal worship in Israel, even though we know that there had always been tendencies towards Baal worship from the very beginning of Israel's settlement in the promised land.

Ahab married Jezebel but did not force her to give up her gods when she moved to Samaria. In fact, he encouraged her to express her faith and to support her tradition. They regularly entertained the priests of Baal in the royal home. Ahab was guilty of the same "sin" as Solomon—tolerating the Baal worship of his wife. For his effort to keep his marriage together, Ahab was condemned and accused of leading the Israelites into idolatry. The incident concerning Naboth and his vineyard was the straw that broke the camel's back for the D narrator (see 1 Kgs 21:1–16). Elijah condemned the royal family for idolatry and for the murder of Naboth. Ahab got a reprieve after he humbled himself before God; but neither he nor Jezebel had an easy death.

Ahab was killed during a battle with the Arameans as he tried to reclaim the city of Ramoth-gilead (see 1 Kgs 22:34–38). And just as Elijah had predicted, the dogs licked up Ahab's blood after he bled to death in his chariot. Before going into battle, Ahab sought the help of Judah's ruler, Jehoshaphat, in his aggressive move against Ben-hadad of Aram. In this instance, we see Judah and Israel putting aside their issues to present a united front. This alliance might have been prompted by the fact that Ahab and Jehoshaphat were in-laws—Ahab's daughter was married to Jehoshaphat's son!

After Jehoshaphat died, his son and Ahab's son were rulers in their respective territories—Jehoram in Judah and Ahaziah in Israel. This section of the text can be a bit confusing—"Jehoram" (or "Joram") is a name shared by two men; the names are variants and are used interchangeably in the text:

- The first Joram refers to Ahab's son, who ruled Israel after his brother, Ahaziah, was assassinated. He got the support of his uncle Jehoshaphat to settle a dispute with the Moabites. He was injured in an attack on Ramoth-gilead and retired to the royal summer home in Jezreel. Jehu, who took over the throne, later assassinated him. This Jehoram was the last of Ahab's sons to rule over Israel.

- The second Jehoram was Jehoshaphat's son, who succeeded his father to rule over Judah. He ruled for eight years and was married to Athaliah, Ahab's daughter. His story is given with more detail in 2 Chronicles 21. We learn that he was the first-born of Jehoshaphat and was given the throne by his father. Jehoram promptly killed his six brothers as well as some other officials of Judah. He had to fight against the Edomites, who tried to declare their independence from Judah. In addition, he was forced to deal with Libnah, which also tried to free itself from Judah's domination. He was said to follow in the ways of the royal family in Israel because he made high places in Judah and led the people of Jerusalem into idolatry (see 2 Chron. 21:12–15). Elijah prophesied that Jehoram's people would suffer a great plague and he would suffer from a disease of the bowels. During his reign, the Philistines and Arabs invaded Jerusalem and took away treasures from the ruler's house, his sons, and their wives. The only son left was his youngest, Jehoahaz (this is a variation of Ahaziah's name). But God did not destroy him because of God's promise to David. Elijah's prophecy, however, came to pass. (Read 2 Chron. 21:18–19a.)

144 ··· **THE DIVIDED TERRITORY**

When Jehoram died, his son, Ahaziah, succeeded him. So, is this as clear as mud? If it is, let me try again to confuse you—"Ahaziah" is also a name shared by two men:

- The first was Ahaziah, ruler of Israel. He reigned for two years over Israel. Early in his reign, he suffered a fall and was seriously injured. Instead of sending for a doctor, he sent a messenger to ask Baal-zebub, the god in Ekron, if he would survive. Ekron was a city in the land of the Philistines. The prophet Elijah heard of Ahaziah's inquiry of Baal and soundly condemned him for this action. Elijah prophesied that Ahaziah would surely die. When Ahaziah's messenger returned home too quickly, he asked why. The messenger shared his interaction with Elijah. Ahaziah sent a captain and fifty soldiers to bring Elijah to the royal home. Not only did Elijah refuse the invitation, he called down fire that burned up the captain and his men. Ahaziah sent another captain and fifty soldiers. Elijah repeated the action and had them burned up, too. A third time, Ahaziah sent a captain and fifty soldiers. Wisely this time, the captain did not command Elijah to follow him; instead, he pled for his life and the lives of his soldiers. An angel advised Elijah to go and talk with the ruler. In their confrontation, Elijah pulled no punches (read 2 Kgs 1:15–16). And King Ahaziah died. He had no sons to inherit the throne, so his brother, Jehoram, succeeded him. This Ahaziah was the uncle of the second Ahaziah.

- The second Ahaziah was the son of King Jehoram of Judah. Ahaziah became ruler of Judah when his father died. He reigned over Judah for one year. Athaliah was his mother. He went with King Joram (or Jehoram) the son of Ahab to fight the Arameans in order to reclaim Ramoth-gilead. Both rulers ended up in Jezreel. While they were together, Elisha was working behind the scenes to anoint and make the ruler a commander of Israel's army, Jehu the son of Jehoshaphat, son of Nimshi (he is so identified so as not to be confused with King Jehoshaphat's family line). Jehu traveled to Jezreel and assassinated both rulers.

So, now that you have all this clearly in your minds—we are talking about uncles, nephews, and in-laws with the same names: Jehoram (Joram) and Ahaziah. Let's see if things become clearer as we move along the story. We will back up and fill in some details. Please be patient because we will get to Athaliah's story. Ahaziah, Ahab's son, ruled over Israel but things started off badly for him. (Read 2 Kgs 1:1.)

He was condemned before he could even get started—instead of sending for a doctor, he sent for help from Baal! Maybe his mother told him to do this; but the result was total condemnation by the prophet Elijah, and so Ahaziah died (see 2 Kgs 1:9–18).

Ahaziah had no sons, so his brother, Jehoram (Joram), assumed the throne in Israel. Jehoram began a reform program in Israel—he removed the pillar of Baal that his father, Ahab, had made, but he is still accused of following the sin of Jeroboam—bad news for him.

King Joram of Israel and King Ahaziah of Judah went up against the Arameans. They followed in the footsteps of their fathers, who helpd each other out in various military campaigns. Unfortunately, Joram was injured and went home to Jezreel to heal (Jezreel was the place of the Naboth incident that further condemned Ahab and Jezebel). Ahaziah went to see how Joram was.

In the meantime, the prophet Elisha had sent a messenger to anoint Jehu the new ruler of Israel. The messenger interrupted a strategy meeting of the commanders, called Jehu outside, and poured oil over him and proclaimed him ruler. When Jehu returned to the meeting, he was forced to share the news with the other army commanders. They gave their consent and affirmation. (Read 2 Kgs 9:11–13.)

Jehu then left for Jezreel. While the two unsuspecting rulers were together, they were told that someone was approaching the city.

The sentinel on watch sent a messenger to find out if the visitor had come in peace. The visitor was Jehu, who hijacked the messenger. The sentinel sent another messenger, who suffered the same fate as the first. The sentinel figured out that something was up and remarked: "It looks like the driving of Jehu son of Nimshi; for he drives like a maniac" (2 Kgs 9:20b).

The rulers then got into their separate chariots and rode outside the city near Naboth's property to meet Jehu. Joram asked if Jehu came in peace. Jehu replies:

> *"What peace can there be, so long as the many whoredoms and sorceries of your mother Jezebel continue?"* (2 Kgs 9:22b)

Joram understood then that Jehu was out to get him for the sins of his idolatrous mother; he turned around to run away from Jehu. Jehu drew his bow and shot Joram in the heart. Jehu instructed his aide, Bidkar, to take Joram out of his chariot and throw him on the ground at Naboth's property—and so the death of Naboth by Jezebel (and Ahab) was avenged. Joram died there.

Ahaziah, no fool, turned and headed towards Beth-haggan. Jehu and his soldiers pursued him. Jehu told his soldiers to shoot Ahaziah. After being wounded, Ahaziah went to Megiddo, where he died.

So on one trip, Jehu killed the ruler of Israel *and* the ruler of Judah! While Jehu was the ruler of Israel, Judah now had no ruler. And we have a dilemma here. God had promised David that he would always have an heir on the throne in Judah. They often failed to live up to the standard he set, but God promised to keep the house of David in leadership in Judah.

This is where the widow Athaliah came in. She learned that her son, Ahaziah, was dead. And she sprung into action. Because there was no leadership in Judah, she took the throne. She had been serving as the queen mother, a position of honor and perhaps some influence. She may have been helping her son rule anyway. It was a small leap for her to assume the crown.

Athaliah's ascent to the throne was problematic for a number of reasons. First of all, she was a woman. And a woman's place was in the home—taking care of domestic matters. Women did not move in a man's world. We know that assertive, smart, ambitious women did not fare well in biblical times. From Eve to Herodias, strong women were condemned and silenced. For Athaliah to dare take the crown was an act that did not deserve to be recognized.

Secondly, she was a foreign woman. Her family ruled in Israel, not Judah; and if it had not been for her husband, she wouldn't even have been in Judah. As an outsider, she had no right to be in any kind of leadership position.

Thirdly, she was a worshipper of Baal—the very god that God had ordered the people to eradicate. Athaliah inherited her faith from her mother, Jezebel, and was a strong supporter of Baal worship. Even the better rulers were criticized for allowing Baal worship and the presence of high places and altars. To think that an actual Baal worshipper could be a leader was absurd.

In fact, the biblical narrative makes it clear that her reign was not legitimate. In every case, the biography of the ruler follows a formula:

- The year of the opposing ruler's reign is given along with his name.
- The name of the ruler is given.
- The age of the ruler and/or the length of his reign is given.
- Some information is given, such as his mother's name.
- An assessment of his leadership is given.
- A reference is made to various acts of the ruler that are listed in another book.
- A death announcement is given as well as where he is buried.
- His successor is named.
- In some instances, a flashback of some act of the ruler is given.

The formula is standard; for example, read 2 Kings 15:1–7, the "biography" of Azariah.

Athaliah's story begins with the matter-of-fact, "Now when . . . ." Her story is almost an aside and certainly not part of the main story. Yet she was the only female monarch in Israel or Judah—although she was not the only woman to serve in this capacity during ancient times; remember that Solomon entertained the Queen of Sheba!

Athaliah assumed the throne on the heels of Jehu's sweeping purge of her family. He killed her son as well as the ruler of Israel. Jehu also went into Jezreel and made sure that Jezebel, Athaliah's mother, was killed. (Read 2 Kgs 9:33–35.)

Jehu sent a letter to the leaders, elders, and guardians of Ahab's sons and grandsons of Jezreel seeking a representative of Ahab's house to defend Ahab's family. When the people heard his challenge, they were afraid—Jehu had already killed two rulers and a queen mother; how could they win against him? Instead of sending a family representative, they pledged allegiance to him and would give him whatever he asked for. And he asked a high price—the heads of all of Ahab's sons—all seventy of them. The people did as he asked. (Read 2 Kgs 10:8–11.)

With his work done in Jezreel, Jehu went to the capital city of Samaria. On the way, he met up with a group of Ahab's relatives at Beth-eked. They were going to Jezreel to see the ruler. Jehu slaughtered them (see 2 Kgs 10:14).

Before he reached Samaria, he met up with Jehonadab, son of Rechab, and invited Jehonadab to join him on his journey and witness his zeal for God. The two reached Samaria. (Read 2 Kgs 10:17.)

After Jehu exterminated the rest of Ahab's family, he called for a grand assembly of Baal worshippers to come to Samaria. The call was sent throughout the territory and people came from miles around to the grand celebration. But Jehu had played a cruel trick on them—after removing any lovers of God, he ordered his soldiers to kill all the worshipers. (Read 2 Kgs 10:24–27.)

Jehu had done what no ruler before him had done in Israel: "Thus Jehu wiped out Baal from Israel" (2 Kgs 10:28). With this statement, we expect his leadership to get a two-thumbs up from the D narrator. Instead, we learn that for all his zeal, Jehu didn't finish the job—he forgot to dismantle the golden calves at Bethel and Dan. For D, these still symbolized the possibility for idolatry. And for this reason, Jehu's endorsement is conditional—he would have a four-generation dynasty, but no more.

It is against the backdrop of Jehu's purge that we find Athaliah assuming the throne. He had destroyed not only her family, but also her religion! Now it was time for her to show him and all of Israel what the real deal was. It is likely that she planned to reestablish Baal worship and implement a different administrative style.

She began her reign by killing any contenders to the royal crown—she killed her remaining relatives to protect her crown. While this is abhorrent, it indicates that she wielded power. She had a military force that fought on her behalf and protected her. She must have had the support of some of Judah's leaders because she ruled for six years. She probably learned leadership from her grandfather, father, mother, and husband. She was a force with which the Judeans had to reckon. We hear nothing of her administration—probably because the narrator did not want us to invest ourselves in her story. Given a chance, she might have proven to be an able leader—she certainly had watched her family members wheel and deal. We should not think that she was incapable of providing competent, if not visionary, leadership, too.

She successfully killed all the competition except for the baby Joash (Jehoash), who was taken, hidden away, and kept safe for six years. The baby was "abducted" by his half sister, Jehosheba. It just so happened that Jehosheba was married to the priest Jehoiada. He conspired against Athaliah and declared Joash ruler of Judah.

Jehoiada devised a fairly complicated plan to install Joash at a time when Athaliah was unable to muster her troops to her side. (Read 2 Kgs 11:5–8.)

The captains and guards followed Jehoiada's orders; they took spears and shields that belonged to David to guard the young son of the ruler and grandson of the queen—Jehoiada led the coronation ceremony in the Temple. They put up such a ruckus that Athaliah heard the commotion and went to investigate. What she saw was astonishing. (Read 2 Kgs 11:14a.)

She tore her clothes as a public sign of mourning. In a last ditch effort, she accused Jehoiada and his cohorts of treason; but the die was cast against Athaliah. Jehoiada did not want to kill her in the Temple and had her escorted outside, where she was killed.

Jehoiada continued the coronation by making a covenant between God, the ruler, and the people. The people went en masse to destroy the remaining vestiges of Baal worship and killed Mattan, the remaining priest of Baal (see 2 Kgs 11:18).

The people then marched the ruler from the Temple into the royal palace where he took his place on the throne. This was a double celebration:

> *So all the people of the land rejoiced; and the city was quiet after Athaliah had been killed with the sword at the ruler's house.* (2 Kgs 11:20)

And so ended the reign of Athaliah.

So what can we say about her leadership? Her reign started in blood and ended with blood—and with a child on the throne. Joash was seven when he became ruler. We presume that Jehoiada was the real power until the child reached adulthood. In the brief biography that we have, we cannot give a full assessment of Athaliah's character or of her leadership. She behaved like the monarchs—she was ruthless and cold-blooded. But she was no worse than they—Solomon and her husband killed their brothers to keep their crowns secure. She was a religious woman and tried to support her faith tradition. She knew how to use and lead the military. She must have had some strategy for gaining the throne in Judah—no one rose up against her to prevent her usurpation of the crown. In this way, she reminds us of Deborah during the time of the judges (see Judges 4–6).

She was a strong woman who knew what she wanted and was not afraid to go after it. In this way, she reminds us of Eve, Delilah, and her mother, Jezebel. It is clear that she loved her son; we suspect that she spent time with him, guiding him in his leadership.

She was a woman of multicultural background. She brought the traditions of her mother and her father to her leadership. She understood royal prerogative and certainly knew how to use power. She was brave enough to play a man's game by men's rules. She did what she had to do in order to get what she wanted. She was not depicted as a temptress, harlot, or helpless woman. She was in charge and the men did what she told them to do.

Unfortunately, we have no other picture of her—and we are left to wonder who this powerful, fearless, ambitious woman was. And we wonder what she might have become if given a chance. The narrator tries to downplay her reign; there is no legitimacy given to her leadership. In spite of the narrator's attempt to silence her—we see her. She was a bold, bodacious, and brave woman. We may not have a full picture of her. But we know that she was doomed from the very beginning. She, however, leaves us with the powerful image of a woman wearing the crown in Judah, in the city of David, in the city where God's name resided. Long live the queen!

REFLECTION QUESTIONS

1. Given the brief description, what kind of leader was Athaliah?
2. What were her leadership strengths? Her leadership weaknesses?
3. In what ways did Athaliah exercise power? In what ways did she exercise authority?
4. What advice would you offer her about her public relations image?

5. Athaliah was a woman alone—no parents, no husband, no sons, no record of daughters or in-laws. What advice would you offer her about building a support system?

6. Athaliah grew up surrounded by violent people. What could she have done to break the cycle of violence?

7. What do you think her grandfather Omri would have said to her about leadership?

8. Can a woman run a nation? Explain your answer.

9. What leadership challenges do you think she would have faced from other nations?

10. Did Athaliah have any redeeming qualities? Explain.

9 · Israel—HOSHEA

I NOW PRONOUNCE THE TERRITORY DEAD!

Read 2 Kings 17:1–6

Hoshea had the dubious distinction of presiding over the death of his territory at the hands of the Assyrians. Israel was more volatile than Judah, mostly because there was no designated dynasty for the territory. In addition, the northern territory was more vulnerable to outside threats because it was part of an international trade route. Israel's history after the split with Judah is filled with assassinations, coups, conspiracies, and mayhem. The monarchs marched through Israel's history in rapid and bloody succession—each judged negatively if he followed in the way of Jeroboam.

Samaria, Israel's capital, was under siege and finally taken by King Sargon II in 721 B.C.E. Assyria had been coming on strong for quite some time before it struck Israel. Assyria was looking for conquests rather than mere vassal states and tributes. Israel was in no condition to fight the superpower—after Jeroboam II's death, the political situation became chaotic. The rulers following him, Zechariah and Shallum, were both assassinated after being in office a mere six months and one month, respectively (see 2 Kgs 15:8–14). It is difficult to know what motivated so much instability—ambition, power, status, or unbridled loyalty.

King Menahem, an assassin himself, was able to stave off Assyria but only by paying heavy taxes to King Tiglath-pileser. Menahem raised money by instituting an extra tax on the wealthier citizens of Israel. His hope was to ingratiate himself to the Assyrian monarch so he would help the ruler of Israel maintain his political hold on the territory. Menahem's actions, however, put the nation in hock to Assyria and began digging a hole out of which the nation would have difficulty climbing.

His son, Pekahiah, succeeded him. He wanted to be held in favor by the Assyrians. But he, too, was assassinated two years into his reign. His assassin was one of his army commanders, Pekah.

Pekah, according to 2 Kings 15:27, reigned for twenty years. He was in cahoots with the ruler of Damascus, Rezin, who may have helped Pekah usurp the throne. Pekah was part of an anti-Assyrian alliance along with Tyre and Philistia. In addition, Pekah entered a war with Judah, further weakening Israel. The King of Assyria, Tiglath-pileser, removed Pekah from his post as ruler and placed Hoshea in charge. Hoshea, the last ruler over Israel, assassinated Pekah. There is no indication that these men were capable of leading a nation, let alone a nation in crisis. They made one big mess in Israel, and its neighbors gained strength.

While Israel continued to maintain an air of internationality, trouble was brewing underneath the surface. The monarchy brought with it some serious economic issues that resulted in sharp class distinctions. The nation, under God's rule, was supposed to exemplify equality and community. Instead, we see the beginnings of categories of people—those who had land and wealth and those who did not. Those with money exploited those who had little. So while some greatly benefited from the monarchy, the average citizens did not fare as well. They had to work hard and sometimes received little or no pay. With the economic and social changes, there were bound to be religious changes as well.

Israel was a much more cosmopolitan state than Judah; Israel had the task of integrating various groups of persons within its realm. We have already seen how intermarriages brought challenges regarding worship and loyalty. The monarchs, who were supposed to walk a narrow line, did nothing to encourage the people to worship YHWH only; rather, they tolerated a wide range of styles and beliefs. Their leniency, which made good political sense, made awful sense according the shapers of the tradition. The priests hired by the state could not be trusted to maintain pure worship of YHWH; prophets often catered to the rulers, telling them what they wanted to hear rather than bringing a message from God.

Israel was the seedbed for class distinctions; we also see the rise of the prophetic office during the monarchy. Samuel was the forerunner in the movement to hold rulers accountable to God and to God's people. Other prophets of the era include Nathan, Elijah, Elisha, Ahijah, Micaiah, Amos and Hosea. They gave scathing indictments of the monarchs who failed to walk in the ways of God and to keep God's statutes and commandments. They failed to follow the way of David. The monarchs just didn't get it, even with ample warning and instruction from the prophets. So much of what the prophets said and did was rooted in God's sovereign rule over the territory—they spoke truth to power, which is never an easy job. They suffered along with the people as they lived out the consequences of their actions and choices.

The monarchs' refusal to listen to the prophets just propelled the nation into deeper despair. And Hoshea did nothing to help matters. We don't know how long Israel could have existed as a vassal state to Assyria. Certainly, the nation was hanging by a slender thread, but it was a thread nonetheless. As the tribute became heavier and more difficult to pay, Hoshea decided to play both ends against the middle. He stopped paying Assyria because he thought Egypt would come to his aid. (Read 2 Kgs 17:3–4.)

Instead of independence, Hoshea was put in a trick bag and Israel was the biggest loser. While he was confined, Hoshea helplessly watched his territory crumble. It took two years for Assyria to conquer Samaria; some suggest that the delay was due to the death of King Shalmaneser V (722 B.C.E.) and other rebellions that sprung up throughout the empire. But Assyria maintained a stronghold on Samaria and the people suffered greatly. While there was no evidence that Assyria sacked the city, the most devastating aspect of the occupation was the deportation of its citizens to places throughout the Assyrian empire. There were a number of such deportations over a period of time. The Assyrians wanted to scatter those it captured to lessen the chance of rebellion; so people were mixed in together who may have had very different worldviews, beliefs, and traditions. In addition, others were imported into Israel, bringing their various traditions, beliefs, and worldviews. Surely, some Israelites found their way south to Judah; but that nation was having its own set of struggles.

Whatever gifts and strengths Hoshea may have had, he was not the man to save Israel. Instead, he sold the nation into bondage and Israel came to an end. In 2 Kings 17, we find a long list of Israel's sins. These were the abominations that led to the fall of Israel and to the Exile:

- Israel continued to worship other gods despite God's intervention on their behalf in Egypt.
- Israel insisted on being like other nations in worship and governance.
- Israel built high places to worship despite the presence of God's name in Jerusalem.
- Israel set up altars and pillars on the high hills and under the green trees.

- Israel offered sacrifices and other rituals on these high places when the Temple was in Jerusalem.
- Israel worshiped idols, which was strictly prohibited.
- Israel turned away from the prophets who brought God's Word.
- Israel worshiped false gods and golden calves and in this way served Baal.
- Israel sold themselves to do evil.
- Israel failed to walk in the way of David and rejected God's chosen earthly ruler.

For these reasons, Israel fell. Perhaps the greatest tragedy was not that Israel fell but that it fell on false hopes. The people lived with the belief that God would not let anything really bad happen to them. Yes, things were rough and many people suffered, but when it really counted, God would step in and save the day. After all, God had done it so many times before. Why should things be different now? This kind of optimism is what faith is all about and we can applaud their faithfulness.

But what made this so tragic was that the people never saw their responsibility in their plight. They didn't see the need to turn from their idolatrous ways and turn back to God. They operated as if they were doing all the right things—they thought God's grace was automatic and required nothing from them.

They ignored the prophets' warnings—each step the monarch took to bolster his ambition or his lust was a step away from God. Those rulers who recognized their sin were able to humble themselves before God—they confessed, repented, and sought forgiveness. But most did not; they looked for scapegoats or thought they could finesse their way out of difficulty. They played games with God and with God's people—and they paid a high price for their indifference.

In many ways, a fall was inevitable. From a theological perspective, Israel was always on shaky ground. With the choice of Jeroboam, Israel sealed its fate.

I think, however, that there are some other important factors to consider. Israel was part of a vast movement of people throughout the ancient Near East—empires rose and fell; monarchs were crowned and deposed; the only constant was change. When the territory split into two nations, it was inevitable that something negative would happen. Israel was a presence of power and might when unified and working together. As separate nations, however, Israel and Judah squabbled among themselves, which only weakened their positions against outside threats. Nations have life cycles just as nature and people do— perhaps, after a golden age under David and Solomon, Israel had reached its zenith and it was time to move off the world stage.

Whatever we may think about its demise, Israel went the way of other nations—a shining star for a while, then a fading out into nothingness.

REFLECTION QUESTIONS

1. Hoshea assumed the throne by violence. Did the end (attaining the crown) justify the means?
2. What were Hoshea's leadership strengths? What were his leadership weaknesses?
3. Dr. Martin L. King Jr. wrote a powerful letter while in jail, "Letter from a Birmingham Jail." What do you think Hoshea wrote while the Assyrian authorities confined him?
4. What was the defining moment for Hoshea's leadership?
5. Have you ever had to shut down a business? Describe the experience. What did you learn from that process?
6. Could Hoshea have saved Israel? Explain.
7. Do you think God treated Israel fairly? Explain.
8. If Hoshea could go back in time, what do you think he would say to David? To Solomon? To Jeroboam?
9. What legacy did Hoshea leave for us?
10. What advice do you think Hoshea offered his counterparts in Judah (Jotham and Ahaz) about the future?

10 · Judah—ZEDEKIAH

IT'S OUR TURN TO DIE!

Read 2 Kings 25:1–7

There are people in Judah who watched the fall of Israel with mixed feelings. No doubt, some felt that Israel got what it deserves. If only they had stayed with Judah. Things were not perfect, but when have they ever been? Despite its size and abundant resources, Israel could not withstand the political and economic tidal waves that washed over it as its territories declared their independence and as Assyria flexed its imperial muscles.

Some in Judah saw the handwriting on the wall as Israel gave in to its citizens who worshiped and adored Baal. Israel's tolerance for diversity and pluralism did not create an atmosphere of freedom but rather created opportunities for God's people to be seduced and enticed into idolatry. The rulers were corrupt themselves, overtaxing the people and allowing the wealthy to exploit and abuse the poor.

The rulers hired priests and prophets to do what the ruler wanted with little regard to what God wanted. With a watered down faith and treacherous political practices and policies, it was inevitable that Israel would reap the bitter fruits of its labor. If only Israel had stayed with Judah, it might have avoided the disaster of seeing the nation in ruins and its people displaced and dispersed through the Assyrian empire. Surely, some in Judah saw Israel's fate as one justified because of Israel's political, economic, and spiritual choices.

Others, no doubt, lamented the fate of their kinfolk and began looking over their own shoulders to see who was creeping up on them. These would recognize that if a nation as strong as Israel with its multiple territorial holdings, with its wealth and resources, with its huge military machine and intellectual acumen, well . . . if Israel could fall, Judah might be next in line.

Now with Israel no more, we focus our attention on Judah to see how they fared in the midst of tremendous change and upheaval.

In the third year of King Hoshea's reign in Israel, Hezekiah became ruler over Judah. It was with great interest that Hezekiah watched the happenings in Israel. Perhaps he took an object lesson from Israel and thought he could keep his territory safe.

Hezekiah made sweeping reforms in Judah—more than any other ruler since the territories split after Solomon's death. He removed the high places, broke down the pillars and cut down the sacred pole. He even went the extra mile and destroyed the bronze serpent that Moses had made. During the wilderness wanderings, Moses had had to deal with the whining and complaining of the people; their murmurings were often justified because of no water or food. But their methods remind us of the tantrums of the "terrible two" phase of childhood. God had an answer for them:

> *Then [YHWH] sent poisonous serpents among the people, and they bit the people, so that many Israelites died.* (Num. 21:6)

The people saw the poisonous snakes as God's punishment for their lack of gratitude for being free and sustained (even if they didn't like the food, they had nourishment, "we detest this miserable food . . ." Num. 21:5b). They confessed their sin of speaking against God and asked Moses to pray on their behalf. Moses did and received an answer from God:

> And [YHWH] said to Moses, "Make a poisonous serpent, and set it on a pole; and everyone who is bitten shall look at it and live." So Moses made a serpent of bronze, and put it upon a pole; and whenever a serpent bit someone, that person would look at the serpent of bronze and live. (Num 21:8–9)

The bronze serpent, or the Nehushtan, became an object of worship. Even this respected symbol of liturgical art was dismantled in Hezekiah's reform.

Hezekiah, then, restored centralized worship in Judah; the people had to come to Jerusalem to worship because the other sites had been dismantled. Furthermore, Hezekiah himself set the example for the people. (Read 2 Kgs 18:5–6.)

Not since the days of David do we find a more pious and sincere ruler—this was the way life should be and Hezekiah was highly praised by the D storyteller. And we are not surprised that things went well for Hezekiah:

> [YHWH] was with him; wherever he went, he prospered. (2 Kgs 18:7a)

Hezekiah still had to deal with the political realities of his day—the Assyrians and the Philistines. His biggest challenge was with the Assyrians. Buoyed by their stunning victory over Israel, the Assyrians now looked to conquer all of Palestine. Nearly twenty years after the takedown of Israel and Samaria, Assyria looked to Judah as the next conquest. The ruler of Assyria was now Sennacherib, who succeeded his father Sargon II, and he was at Jerusalem's doorstep.

Hezekiah is believed to have been part of an anti-Assyrian movement of vassal states that withheld tribute to the superpower. Assyria had no choice but to get the wayward nations back on track, to make them recognize who the real power was. But Hezekiah was no dummy; he took a course of action that made Judah stronger against outside threats. He built a network of tunnels that brought water into the city of Jerusalem. This public works project, the Siloam tunnel, meant that the city would have water if it was blockaded.

Second, Hezekiah knew how to play the political game. When Sennacherib marched against Jerusalem, Hezekiah confessed that he had made a mistake by withholding tribute. He told the ruler of his willingness to make restitution. (Read 2 Kgs 18:14.)

Hezekiah delivered the goods: all the silver from the Temple and palace as well as gold stripped from the very doors and doorposts of the Temple. But Sennacherib would not be shown up by a vassal state and sent three representatives to put Hezekiah and his people in their place. The showdown was dramatic and tense. Sennacherib sent a sizeable military contingent to Jerusalem along with three of his heavy hitters:

- The Tartan, who, after the ruler, was the highest ranking official of the Assyrian empire
- The Rabsaris, literally "chief of the eunuchs," a high ranking military administrator who went on military missions with the Tartan and who might have been the commander-in-chief
- The Rabshakeh, the chief diplomat and negotiator, an eloquent and skilled speaker who thoroughly understood his ruler's vision

Not to be outdone, Hezekiah sent his own trio of negotiators:

- Eliakim son of Hilkiah, who was the palace chief of staff
- Shebnah, who was the keeper of royal records and understood the politics of the day
- Joah son of Asaph, who was the chief recorder

Hezekiah sent his highest-ranking Judahite officials to verbally battle with the Assyrian taskforce. Let the games begin!

The Rabshakeh set forth a persuasive argument designed to melt the hearts of the people so they would give in without the use of force. Words were cheap and would not save Judah; furthermore:

- Judah would not survive if it thought Egypt could help; Egypt was only a shadow of its former self and could not help anyone, not even itself (2 Kgs 18:21).

- Judah would not survive if it thought YHWH would deliver the nation. There may have been a chance, but when Hezekiah destroyed the high places, it weakened the nation. The people were upset that they were forced to worship only in Jerusalem—what God would tolerate that? Internal discontent with Hezekiah's reform only helped Assyria (2 Kgs 18:22).

- Judah would not survive if it thought it had the military strength to take on Assyria. The people were so frustrated that even if Assyria gave Judah two thousand horses, Hezekiah would not be able to find two thousand men to ride them against Assyria (2 Kgs 18:23–24).

- Judah would not survive simply because Assyria was doing God's work against Judah:

Moreover, is it without [YHWH] that I have come up against this place to destroy it? [YHWH] said to me, "Go up against this land, and destroy it." (2 Kgs 18:25)

The Rabshakeh, in essence, told Hezekiah's officials that Judah should surrender—it was God's will for them to fall to Assyria. Despite Hezekiah's sweeping and thorough reforms, it was too late for Judah. There was nothing they could do—Assyria would win the day.

Eliakim, Shebnah, and Joah understood the Rabshakeh's play to undermine the people's confidence and to instill fear in them.

Hezekiah's men requested that the Assyrian officials speak in Aramaic rather than Hebrew. The people would not understand Aramaic and would be left out of the conversation. Aramaic was the international language of diplomacy and trade. But the Rabshakeh knew exactly what he was doing and even accused the trio of Judah of deliberately trying to keep the people ignorant. (Read 2 Kgs 18:27.)

The Rabshakeh shouted in the language of the people and gave them a powerful word:

- "Do not let Hezekiah deceive you." He can't protect you (2 Kgs 18:29).

- "Do not let Hezekiah make you rely on [YHWH]." God can't help you now (2 Kgs 18:30).

- "Do not listen to Hezekiah." Your help is now in King Sennacherib who will bring you into a real promised land—a land where there is plenty food and drink (2 Kgs 18:30–32).

- "Do not listen to Hezekiah when he misleads you by saying [YHWH] will deliver you"—no one gets by Assyria. Where are the other gods who tried to deliver their people from the Assyrians? Exactly—they did nothing; so don't even think that your God will do any better! (2 Kgs 18:33–35).

The Rabshakeh was a great preacher and he made perfect sense. Sennacherib was their new god. YHWH had not delivered on the divine promise of protection—but Sennacherib could and would, if the people followed him! On the surface, he was exactly right and one is hard-pressed to refute his argument. In reaction to these words, Hezekiah could only tear his clothes in mourning. The Assyrian negotiator had done his job—Hezekiah's envoy reported back to the ruler and they all went into mourning. What to do? What to do??

Hezekiah, ever the pious ruler, did the only thing he could— he went to the Temple to pray. In addition, he sent Eliakim, Shebnah, and the senior priests to the prophet Isaiah with the sad news and to ask for prayers. Judah was in a bad situation—and the future looked grim.

Surely the people were fearful—how did things get to this point? Hezekiah was depressed and puzzled—he had done everything right, so where was God now? The covenant deal was on shaky ground—Hezekiah had gotten the people back on track. God had promised to protect them, to keep a descendant of David on the throne, and to keep the city where God's name resided safely—so what was up with this mess with Assyria?

Isaiah essentially told Hezekiah's leadership team, "Hold on—it ain't over yet." (Read 2 Kgs 19:6–7.)

God had heard the Assyrians' taunts and barbs—and God had something for them. Not to worry, God said, Sennacherib would soon be on his way home and away from Judah.

When the Assyrian ruler heard that King Tirhakan of Ethiopia (Cush) was rebelling against him, Sennacherib did a curious thing. Instead of going to take care of business, he sent a letter to Hezekiah. Sennacherib made it clear that this tactic would not work. In essence, he said that other gods had tried to foil him and failed. YHWH would be no exception to this. "Don't even think about it—Judah *will* belong to Assyria," the ruler said.

Hezekiah's response was a plea to God—"Are you going to take this? Are you a God who is bullied by the likes of this arrogant human ruler? Are you going to give us up because you are wimp?"

Of course, I'm exaggerating, but Hezekiah was as bewildered as we are about the turn of events. (Read 2 Kgs 19:14b–19.)

Hezekiah was distressed, distraught, and depressed—but Isaiah had another word from God—"Do not despair; it still ain't over yet!" God would not let Judah be taken by Assyria. After three years, the nation would be back to its old self (see 2 Kgs 19:21–31). In fact, that very night, God struck down 185,000 in Sennacherib's camp. The Assyrian ruler returned home to Nineveh and, while he was worshipping, he was killed by his own sons. After his two murderous sons fled into the land of Ararat, his son Esar-haddon succeeded him (2 Kgs 19:37).

Hezekiah's trust in God was not in vain. God, indeed, delivered Judah. This was cause for celebration and rejoicing—God reigned. But Judah's celebration should have been tempered—this was just the beginning of Judah's troubles.

Hezekiah was faced with a death-dealing illness from which he recovered because of his prayer to God. Isaiah informed him that God had granted him fifteen more years (2 Kgs 20:1–11). Hezekiah received a get-well wish and gift from Merodach-baladan, the ruler of Babylon. Hezekiah, somewhat foolishly, gave the ruler's messengers a tour of the Judahite treasury and storehouses. Isaiah prophesied that what they had seen, they would take for Babylon in the days to come (2 Kgs 20:12–21). Hezekiah surprises us all with his inner response—since the event would happen in the future, he didn't have to worry; his reign would be untainted. Hezekiah was not concerned about future generations. Despite his love for God and his extensive religious reforms, in the end, it was all about Hezekiah (see 2 Kgs 20:19b).

These episodes in Hezekiah's reign are foreshadowings of Judah's demise. Judah was dodging bullets but it remained to be seen how long the nation could survive like this. Assyria was strong and mighty, but even now Babylon was growing. Hezekiah's good relationship with Babylon seemed like a good thing—but we will see how it turned out.

The shadows began to deepen with the reign of Hezekiah's son, Manasseh. He ruled Judah for fifty-five years—just enough time to undo all of his father's reforms. Manasseh rebuilt the high places, erected altars for Baal, made a sacred pole, and worshiped and served other gods! Not only that, Manasseh engaged in the forbidden acts of foreign gods: he practiced child sacrifice by making his sons pass through fire; practiced soothsaying and augury; dealt with mediums and wizards; and put carved images of Asherah in the Temple of God! Did this man not pay attention to anything his father did?

It may be that Manasseh gave in to the pressure of those who felt that Hezekiah's reforms were problematic and extreme. But if

Hezekiah's reforms were over the top, so were Manasseh's attempts to bring balance. So heinous were his actions that he left God no choice in dealing with Judah. (Read 2 Kgs 21:12b–15.)

To add insult to injury, Manasseh's son was no better than he was—Amon continued to lead Judah into idolatry. He abandoned God and walked in the way of Manasseh. Now that Judah was walking in the way of Israel, we expect dire consequences for the southern territory. Once a beacon of faithfulness and obedience to God, Judah was now creating space in God's temple for Baal! There could be no excuse for such actions.

As horrendous as his deeds were, Manasseh was redeemed in the book of Chronicles. In this later tradition, Manasseh was imprisoned by the ruler of Assyria and taken to Babylon. While in captivity, Manasseh prayed to God, who heard his plea and restored him to Jerusalem and to his territory. Manasseh was converted to the worship of YHWH. Manasseh reversed his sacrilege against God by taking the foreign gods out of the Temple, tearing down all the altars to Baal, restoring God's altar in the Temple, offering sacrifices of thanksgiving, and commanding the people to worship God only. Manasseh did not, however, dismantle the high places and thus did not recentralize worship to Jerusalem (see 2 Chron. 33:3–17). But 2 Kings does not offer us a redeeming picture of him.

Surely, Hezekiah was turning—no, he must have been spinning—in his grave over the work of his son and his grandson.

His servants assassinated Amon after only two years in office. The people, though, murdered Amon's murderers and placed Josiah on the throne (2 Kings 21:19–24).

In Josiah, Judahite leadership regained its senses. Josiah set about to rebuild Jerusalem and the Temple. He mapped out a plan to pay the workers who would do the work. Before the plan was implemented, Hilkiah, the high priest, discovered a copy of "the book of the law." There was no information about how he discovered the book. Hilkiah gave the book to Shaphan, who informed Josiah about the book and read it to him. Shaphan did not indicate either how or where the book was discovered; Josiah didn't ask any questions. Josiah tore his clothes as an act of mourning, perhaps recognizing how far off the mark Judah had fallen (2 Kings 22:8–11).

In order to make sure he understood the importance of the discovery, Josiah sent a group of officials to consult with a respected prophet. Josiah sends Hilkiah the high priest, Ahikam son of Shaphan, Achbor son of Micaiah, Shaphan the secretary, and Asaiah the ruler's servant—a contingent of important leaders in Judah. This was no small matter and Josiah sent the most trusted and respected members of his leadership team.

They went to consult with a prophet who happened to be a woman. Huldah was carefully identified as a trusted and competent prophet as well as a loyal member of Josiah's extended staff. She confirmed Josiah's worse fears—yes, Jerusalem and its people would face judgment because they had disobeyed God by serving idols. There was nothing to be done about the transgression—Judah must play the hand it had. As for Josiah personally, he would die in relative peace before the devastation occurred.

Judah's delegation reported back to Josiah. They did not question Huldah's prophecy and neither did Josiah. Huldah's gender seemed not to have been an issue, a sign that female prophets were commonplace—hooray for women!

Josiah moved forward with his reforms, even if they would not reverse the verdict against the territory. He began by assembling the people—the elders, the priests, the prophets, and all the people—both small and large. He read the "book of the covenant," which was the same book Hilkiah brought to his attention. Josiah conducted a covenant renewal ceremony and the people recommitted themselves to the covenant (2 Kgs 23:1–3).

Josiah commanded Hilkiah the high priest, his associate priests, and the guardians of the threshold to cleanse the Temple of all vestiges of Baal, which are taken outside the city and burned. Josiah had the houses of the male temple prostitutes dismantled;

tore down the altars on the high places; dismantled the altar at Bethel; removed all the shrines of the high places in the towns of Samaria (the now defunct nation Israel was renamed Samaria; its inhabitants were not called Israelites anymore, but Samaritans— these changes in names occurred after the ruler of Assyria took over Israel; he attempted to wipe out their very identity). Josiah had all the priests of the high places captured and killed. After his purge of the land, Josiah returned to Jerusalem. He is ruthless and zealous in his reform efforts—his reforms reach back to the days of Solomon, Jeroboam and Manasseh.

Josiah also reinstituted the Passover festival—reaching back to the days of the Exodus and Joshua (see Exod. 12:1–28 and Josh. 5:10–12). Instead of celebrating the festival in individual homes, Jerusalem was the new site for observing the Passover (so, in the New Testament, in the days of Jesus, we read how all the people gathered at Jerusalem to celebrate the Passover). (Read 2 Kgs 23:21–23.) But Judah's spiritual renewal program did not stop the judgment on Judah. (Read 2 Kgs 23:27.)

Josiah learned that Pharaoh Neco, the ruler of Egypt, was meeting with the ruler of Assyria. The two rulers were meeting to map out a strategy to stop the aggressive moves of Babylon. Josiah tried to meet up with them at Megiddo, a major fortified city; but Neco killed Josiah. His dead body was transported back to Jerusalem where he was buried in his own tomb. The D storyteller was not concerned with the details of Josiah's death so we cannot say why he even made the trip that resulted in his assassination or why Neco of Egypt killed him.

Judah hurled rapidly towards its fate, and it was not a fun ride. After Josiah died, his son Jehoahaz was placed on the throne despite the fact that he was not the eldest son. Egypt controlled Judah and, after three months, King Jehoahaz was captured and deported to Riblah by Pharaoh Neco. Jehoahaz was moved to Egypt where he died (2 Kgs 23:32–34). There is a touch of irony here as we remember the journey of the people out of Egypt.

The Egyptian Pharaoh replaced Jehoahaz with Josiah's oldest son, Eliakim. Pharaoh changed the name of Judah's ruler to Jehoiakim. Now, instead of God choosing a ruler and having a prophet anoint him, Pharaoh appointed one! Jehoiakim reigned over Judah for eleven years. In order to pay the tribute that Egypt required, he heavily taxed the people.

The shadow of Babylon began to loom larger and more menacingly during Jehoiakim's reign. Babylon was ruled by King Nebuchadnezzar. His father was Nabopolassar, the founder of the Chaldean dynasty. Nebuchadnezzar was lauded as the longest reigning and most powerful of the Babylonian monarchs. His territory was Babylonia and the capital city was Babylon. His son, Evil-merodach, succeeded Nebuchadnezzar.

Jehoiakim was by now just a vassal of Egypt. When Egypt lost a decisive battle with Babylonia at Carchemish, Nebuchadnezzar took over Judah and the rest of Egypt's holdings in the area (2 Kgs 24:7). Jehoiakim and Judah belonged to Babylon for three years. When the Babylonians were defeated shortly after the three-year mark, Jehoiakim reestablishes his loyalty with Egypt. But his move was shortsighted because Nebuchadnezzar regrouped and things would never be the same for Judah.

Nebuchadnezzar sent a military coalition against Judah—the Chaldeans, the Arameans, the Moabites, and the Ammonites—and Judah didn't stand a chance. Such a massive strike was not warranted by Judah's size or reputation. This over-the-top coalition was God's work. (Read 2 Kgs 24:3-4.)

For the D storyteller, God was in control of Judah's destiny; the invading troops would extract retribution for Manasseh's blatant disregard for God. Because no details are given, we are left to presume that Jehoiakim died during the Babylonian invasion (2 Kgs 24:6). His son, Jehoiachin, succeeded him.

Jehoiachin reigned over Judah for three months. Nebuchadnezzar sent his army to take Jerusalem. As his soldiers were in the process of taking the city, the ruler himself made a personal appearance. Seeing the handwriting on the wall, Jehoiachin turned himself over to Nebuchadnezzar, who gladly carried out the capture. Not only that, Nebuchadnezzar took Jehoiachin's immediate family, palace staff, temple and palace treasures, and the elite citizens and carted them off to Babylon. (Read 2 Kgs 24:14–16.)

What a sad day for Judah as the people watched Nebuchadnezzar raid Jerusalem of its people and its treasures. The city of David had been violated and the cream of the crop deported to a foreign land. The house of God had been violated and its treasures—silver, gold, and fine vessels—confiscated and exported to Babylon. Surely David and Solomon were spinning in their graves!

Nebuchadnezzar appointed Mattaniah ruler over Judah. Mattaniah, whose name was changed to Zedekiah, was the younger brother of Jehoahaz; he was also Jehoiachin's uncle.

Zedekiah was the last ruler of Judah. He "reigned" for eleven years. He was a mere figurehead because the Babylonians controlled Judah. He rebelled against Nebuchadnezzar, perhaps hoping to join alliances with other nations to overthrow the super powerful Babylonians. But no help was forthcoming—Nebuchadnezzar had had enough of the troublesome Judah. (Read 2 Kgs 25:1–2.)

It took a year and a half finally to take Jerusalem. In the meantime, the people suffered through war against the city as well as a famine. When the city walls were breached, Zedekiah and his soldiers attempted to escape. But they were caught in the plains of Jericho; his army deserted Zedekiah. He was taken to Riblah, where Nebuchadnezzar sentenced him. He was forced to watch as Nebuchadnezzar killed his sons; then his own eyes were put out. The blind ruler of Judah was transferred to Babylon—long live the king.

Yet, this as not the end for Judah. King Nebuchadnezzar sent his bodyguard and henchman, Nebuzaradan, to Jerusalem to take care of some unfinished business—to destroy the city:

- The Temple that David had wanted to build as a suitable house for God and that Solomon took seven years to build and that was made with the finest imported materials—this Temple where God chose to house God's name—was burned down!

- The ruler's palace and all the houses of the royal court—some of which were larger than the Temple and also made of the finest materials—were burned down!

- The wall around Jerusalem was broken down—signaling to the world that Jerusalem was no longer a legitimate city!

- Large numbers of people were carried from Judah into exile—leaving behind only the poorest folks to work and labor for their Babylonian captors!

- The bronze pillars and stands in the Temple were broken and carted off to Babylon!

- The pots, shovels, snuffers, dishes for incense, fire pans, basins, bronze vessels used in worship, and all the accoutrements of the Temple were dismantled and shipped off to Babylon!

To add further insult to injury, Nebuchadnezzar took Seraiah the chief priest, Zephaniah the second priest, the three guardians of the threshold, the army commander, five royal council men, the secretary who commanded the army, and sixty men of the city to Riblah to stand before Nebuchadnezzar. He struck them dead.

Nebuchadnezzar had taken Jerusalem and utterly destroyed it. He appointed Gedaliah as governor over Judah. Judah was no longer a territory—it was a province of Babylon. Provinces don't get rulers—they get appointed a governor—how the mighty had fallen!

The remaining officials from Jerusalem met with Governor Gedaliah at Mizpah. Gedaliah voiced the note of hopelessness. (Read 2 Kgs 25:24.)

Gedaliah encouraged those left in Judah to forget about serving God—serve Nebuchadnezzar—he was their only hope! But Gedaliah's words rang hollow against the backdrop of the next action. (Read 2 Kgs 25:25.)

Perhaps, the saddest words in the story of the biblical monarchs are these . . .

> *Then all the people, high and low and the captains of the*
> *forces set out and went to Egypt; for they were afraid of*
> *the Chaldeans.* (2 Kgs 25:26)

Remember that the Hebrew people had once been slaves in Egypt. Their taskmasters had been mean, cruel, and abusive. The people had cried out because they were so oppressed. God had heard their cry, had compassion for them, and had begun the process of liberation on their behalf. Through the hands, heart, and mind of Moses, God delivered the people out of Egypt—to create in them a people who would be a light to the nations. And here they were, through the smoke and ashes of their burning city—trudging their way back to Egypt—how the mighty have fallen, indeed!

It would be enough to end our story here—here with the acrid smell of smoke offending our nostrils and burning our tearing eyes. What the people dreaded most had come to pass—God had forsaken the very people God called out of bondage:

> *So Israel was exiled from their own land to Assyria until*
> *this day.* (2 Kgs 17:23b)
> *So Judah went into exile out of its land.* (2 Kgs 25:21b)

How was God to be trusted given this outcome? Where was the God who heard and moved with compassion? Where was the God who promised David an eternal dynasty? Where was the God who changed God's mind and dispensed mercy?

The D storyteller does not explicitly tell us where this God was; nor are we given any clues about God's reaction to all this. The storyteller leaves us with one last event. (Read 2 Kgs 25:27–30.)

David's house was not dead. David's descendant, Jehoiachin, was forgotten by some but was remembered by Nebuchadnezzar's son Evil-merodach in Babylon. Jehoiachin was released from prison and treated well by the Babylonians—and so, what might God do with this turn of events?

REFLECTION QUESTIONS

1. This chapter is about the leadership vacuum in Judah. As you think about the succession of rulers, was there any way they could have avoided destruction by Babylon?

2. Have you ever been asked to do an impossible job? How did you handle the situation?

3. What leadership checks and balances are required for a viable working situation?

4. Zedekiah had a vision but no power. What leadership advice would you offer him?

5. What advice would David offer Zedekiah?

6. Why do you think the reforms of Hezekiah and Josiah made no difference in the outcome for Judah?

7. Describe the character of God in these chapters leading up to the downfall of Judah?

8. How do you determine when it is time to leave a job?

9. What kind of exit strategy would have helped Zedekiah?

10. The people of Judah never thought that God would abandon Jerusalem. What is our responsibility and how much should we leave to God?

CLOSING WORD

What a journey we have taken. This path was strewn with dead and violated bodies, with homes raided and desecrated, with powerful men and women abusing power, and a God who seemed to be absent more than present. We must remember that the storyteller of these narratives brought a particular perspective to the events in question. The storyteller was only interested in how the events fit into that agenda.

The aims of D in the books of Samuel and Kings were fourfold:

- To show how the monarchy was established in Israel
- To show how God established an eternal dynasty with David
- To show how idolatry and politics moved the division of the territory along
- To show how the monarchs of both territories dealt with their covenant responsibilities and obligations

The D tradition sought to interpret the events that led to the exile and the beginnings of the Diaspora. The questions they sought to answer are the questions that haunt us, too:

- What happened?
- Who is to blame?
- Can we believe in and trust God while at the same time blame God for the situation of exile and dispersion?
- Where is God in the midst of pain and suffering?
- Must we blame ourselves for how things turn out?

The recurring phrase for both Israel and Judah is a heart-breaker: "If only we had done the right thing for the right reasons . . ."

The nation ended up just like the other nations—the experiment with monarchy was a failure. Samuel's concerns played out in tragic ways for the people of Israel and Judah. (Read 1 Sam. 8:10–18.)

We began our study with the plight of Hannah—yearning for sustenance in the midst of barrenness. We close our study with the plight of God's people—yearning for sustenance in a barren land of exile. We started with no hope and we end with no hope. In between Hannah's prayer at Shiloh and the release of Jehoiachin from prison in Babylon, we experience unspeakable violence, brutality, deceit, international espionage, and downright terror. This is the story of God's people who sought to find a space in the land God promised them when they were nothing but slaves in Egypt.

This has been a roller coaster ride—highs and lows. The consequences of these stories reverberated to the days of Jesus as the people waited for God to keep God's promises—to keep a descendant of David on the throne and to never abandon Jerusalem. As our study ends, we don't know if God will come through; only with the appearance of John the Baptist do we dare hope again. In Jesus, we realize that God does, indeed, keep promises and keeps hope alive.

The Deuteronomic historian tells us a story from a particular perspective. As we continue reading the Bible, we hear the same story over and over again:

- We hear the same story from the perspective of the prophets, who tell us that God is Redeemer and Judge; that we are responsible for our choices and decisions; that God still loves us in spite of ourselves; that life is not always fair; that God is always hanging around somewhere. There is much we hear from Amos, Hosea, Isaiah, Jeremiah, Ezekiel, Elijah, and others.

- We hear the same story from the psalmists who put into liturgical and poetic language the reality of exile and the despair that attends it—that it is okay to acknowledge and feel our pain; to rail against God because of our suffering; to humble ourselves before God and ask to be forgiven; to praise God for our blessings and for lessons learned through pain.

- We hear the same story from the writers of the New Testament, who reassure us that God never leaves us alone and that God will yet be gracious and merciful and forgiving and loving—even to those of us who wonder if we are worthy.

Through these difficult stories that stretch the limits of our belief and faith in a loving and just God, in a God who is on the side of the oppressed, we are forced to consider our own faith. Can it be that God really does love us and wants to be connected to us? Can it be that when we mess up big time, there is still room for divine forgiveness and compassion?

Well, friends, I think it comes down to this. We cannot predict what God will do or what God should do. We cannot know what God will use to save us, instruct us, keep us, challenge us. There are no easy answers. There are no magical formulas to make life easy. There are no set rules that take us on the path to happiness. We must struggle and wrestle with how we live our lives. We are accountable for our choices. We must live through the consequences of our decisions. While we are too much like the nations that surrounded our biblical ancestors, we still must make choices. The adventure in life is not that we always have the answers—the adventure is that answers are possible. In the tension between uncertainty and knowing lies the creative and infinite possibility that we might see something, feel something, taste something, discover something—something miraculous and wonderful, something meaningful and grace-filled, something that delivers us from death and despair.

The D storyteller phrases it as a simple choice:

> *[God says] See, I have set before you today life and prosperity, death and adversity. I call heaven and earth to witness against you today that I have set before you life and death, blessings and curses. Choose life so that you and your descendants may live . . . (Deut. 30:15, 19b)*

And ultimately, we must find it within ourselves to answer bravely, no matter what happens:

> *"Now if you are unwilling to serve [YHWH], choose this day whom you will serve, whether the gods your ancestors served in the region beyond the River or the gods of the Amorites in whose land you are living; but as for me and my household, we will serve [YHWH]." (Josh. 24:15)*

Blessings!

SUGGESTIONS FOR TEACHING AND PREACHING THE MISBEHAVIN' MONARCHS

TEACHING

The Bible contains some of the most interesting and memorable stories found in all of literature. Some of these stories are quite familiar—the stories of Samuel and Saul, for instance. Of others, we may know bits and pieces but have not studied them in a systematic or intentional way—so we may know the story of David and Goliath and David and Bathsheba, but not the stories of David and Abner or David and Joab. Now that we have had the opportunity to explore the stories and lives of selected biblical monarchs, how do we go about the task of preaching and teaching about them? How do we move beyond the entertainment value and object lessons of these tales? Are there ways we can move beyond the superficial and stereotypical to explore their deeper meanings and lessons for us today? Most of the monarchs do not serve as perfect role models— there is so much gore and blood in these stories that it is easier to ignore them. How do we recognize their human frailties and flaws without demonizing them? All of their stories have something to teach us—about valor, courage, creativity, faithfulness, obedience, and love as well as about egotism, selfishness, fear, deception, doubt, and despair.

A major aim of this book is to make the stories accessible and meaningful. The following teaching ideas can be interchanged among the stories and should be attempted after studying the appropriate unit in the book. The exercises are designed to answer the following questions:

- Who are the "characters" in the story?
- What is the action of the story?
- What examples of leadership and/or moral challenges are presented in the story?
- Who speaks and who is silent? What do these actions mean?
- What do we feel and think as we enact the story?
- How is the challenge resolved? What other questions are raised by the story?
- What can we learn about leadership and ourselves from the story?

I hope that these stories will inspire, encourage, and challenge us. How can we read these stories so that we explore our own leadership styles, issues, and concerns? How do we use these stories to delve deeper into who we are as children of God and disciples of Christ? How can these stories deepen our commitment to serve God and humanity through our leadership, ministry, and mission? What can we take from these stories that will help us along our journeys?

Suggested activities might include:

- Stage a courtroom scene placing one of the monarchs on trial or before a Senate hearing—for war crimes, for overstepping protocol, for breaching peace treaties.

- Sponsor a dinner honoring one of the monarchs—it can be serious or a "roast"—and determine who will speak and what they will say.
- Create a tourism website for each of the territories, Judah and Israel—highlight sights and activities for visitors.
- Write funeral services for various characters—Athaliah, Absalom, Rizpah, Nebuchadnezzar—including music, readings, eulogy, obituary, pall bearers, and so on.
- Create debates between unlikely characters—Samuel and Pharaoh Neco; Abigail and Athaliah; Bathsheba and Abishag; David and Josiah; God and Saul.

PREACHING

Effective preaching requires study, reflection, and attention to public speaking. Each preacher brings her or his own methods of sermon development and I encourage you to do what works for you. Every preacher, however, should start with the text itself by reading it! Use a good, reliable translation; I prefer the New Revised Standard Version (NRSV). I always consult more than one translation and version, however, paying attention to differences in wording, ordering, punctuation, and the like. Then, I ask a series of questions of the text including the following:

- What is the text saying? What are the details of the story?
- Who are the participants in the story? What is said about the participants—what can we know about them?
- Who speaks and what does s/he say?
- Who is silent? Why?
- What is the setting that has given rise to this particular text?
- What is happening in the text? Who acts and what does she or he do? What are the issues involved? How are the issues resolved?
- Who reacts in the text? How? Why?

- What happens before and after this particular text? How does this text fit into the larger text?
- Are there any other biblical texts that relate to this particular text? Where? Under what circumstances are there connections?
- What senses (sight, sound, smell, taste, etc.) are aroused by the text?
- What emotions are evoked?
- How can we connect to the text today?
- What is God doing in the text? Why? To what end does God act?
- What is believable in the text? What raises doubt?
- Who in the Bible will disagree with this particular text? What would she or he say instead?
- Who in the church will disagree with this text? What would she or he say instead?
- How does this text fit into God's wider purposes for creation and humanity?
- What does the text say about our lives and world today?
- What does the text call us to be or to do? What prevents us from fulfilling the text's call? What will happen if we fail to heed the text's call? What will happen if we fulfill the text's call?

These and other questions can be asked before any other sources are consulted. This method helps the preacher to see the text before his or her opinions are colored by the opinions of others. Only after wrestling with questions like these is the preacher ready to move on to study aids. Now the preacher is ready to let the sermon unfold.

Themes for preaching might include the following:

- Where is God in a world filled with pain, suffering, anguish, and anxiety?
- What do we do when we feel that God has abandoned us?
- What is the relationship between religion and politics?

- Is it possible to find hope in even the most horrendous situations?
- How do we see and deal with an angry God?
- How do we make ethical choices in our everyday lives?
- How can we be "in" the world without being "of" the world?
- How are we to make sense of the brutality in these narratives?
- For people who are obsessed with feeling good, how do we understand that God is also Judge?
- What is on the other side of loss, failure, and grief? What is the role of faith?
- What does God say about the senseless violence of our day?
- How do we understand the image of God as warrior in our time?
- Can social change happen through revolution and/or violence?
- How do we worship in the midst of despair?

I hope that the reflection questions for each unit serve to stimulate some thinking about how these stories can be used in the church. I am sure that you have some creative ways of preaching and teaching these misbehaving biblical monarchs. I hope these suggested activities and themes will spark your imagination and unlock the stories so that they can bless us.

RESOURCES FOR FURTHER STUDY

Achtemeier, Paul J. General Editor. *Harper's Bible Dictionary*. San Francisco: Harper & Row, 1985.

Balentine, Samuel E. "The Prophet as Intercessor: A Reassessment." *Journal of Biblical Literature* 103/2 (1984): 161–73.

Bell, Derrick. *Ethical Ambition: Living a Life of Meaning and Worth.* New York: Bloomsbury, 2002.

Birch, Bruce C. *The First and Second Books of Samuel: Introduction, Commentary, and Reflections.* Vol. 2 of *The New Interpreter's Bible.* Nashville: Abingdon Press, 1989.

Blair, Christine Eaton. *The Art of Teaching the Bible: A Practical Guide for Adults.* Louisville: Geneva Press, 2001.

Branch, Robin Gallaher. "David and Joab: United by Ambition." *Bible Review*, 19, no. 4 (August 2003): 14–23, 62–63.

Bright, John. *A History of Israel*, 3rd ed. Philadelphia: Westminster Press, 1981.

Brueggemann, Walter. *David's Truth in Israel's Imagination and Memory.* Philadelphia: Fortress Press, 1988.

_____. First and Second Samuel. *Interpretation: A Bible Commentary for Teaching and Preaching*. Louisville: John Knox Press, 1990.

DePree, Max. *Leadership Is an Art*. New York: Dell Publishing, 1989.

Essex, Barbara J. *Bad Boys of the Bible: Exploring Men of Questionable Virtue*. Cleveland: Pilgrim Press, 2003.

_____. *Bad Girls of the Bible: Exploring Women of Questionable Virtue*. Cleveland: Pilgrim Press, 1999.

Exum, J. Cheryl. *Tragedy and Biblical Narrative: Arrows of the Almighty*. New York: Cambridge University Press, 1992.

Good, Robert M. "The Just War in Ancient Israel." *Journal of Biblical Literature*, 104/3 (1985): 385–400.

Green, Barbara, O.P. *King Saul's Asking*. Interfaces Series, ed. Barbara Green, O.P. Collegeville, Minn.: Liturgical Press, 2003.

Halpern, Baruch. *David's Secret Demons: Messiah, Murderer, Traitor, Ruler*. Grand Rapids: William B. Eerdmans, 2001.

Johnson, Spencer. *Who Moved My Cheese? An A-Mazing Way to Deal with Change in Your Work and in Your Life*. New York: G.P. Putnam's Sons, 1998.

Kirsch, Jonathan. *King David: The Real Life of the Man Who Ruled Israel*. New York: Ballantine Press, 2000.

Klein, Lillian R. *Michal, the Barren Wife*. Samuel and Kings: A Feminist Companion to the Bible. 2nd series. Ed. Athalya Brenner. Sheffield, England: Sheffield Academic Press, 2000.

_____. *Bathsheba Revealed*. Samuel and Kings: A Feminist Companion to the Bible. 2nd series. Ed. Athalya Brenner. Sheffield, England: Sheffield Academic Press, 2000.

Lee, Harris W., *Effective Church Leadership: A Practical Sourcebook*. Minneapolis: Augsburg, 1989.

McKenzie, Vashti M. *Not without a Struggle: Leadership Development for African American Women in Ministry*. Cleveland: United Church Press, 1996.

Matthews, Victor H. *Old Testament Turning Points: The Narratives That Shaped a Nation*. Grand Rapids: Baker Academic, 2005.

Muffs, Yochanan. "Agent of [YHWH], Warrior for the People: The Prophet's Paradox." *Bible Review* 18, no. 6 (December 2002): 21–27, 56.

Nelson, Richard D. *First and Second Kings: Interpretation.* In James Luther Mays, ed. Patrick D. Miller, Jr., Old Testament ed. *A Bible Commentary for Teaching and Preaching.* Louisville: John Knox Press, 1987.

Rudman, D. "The Commissioning Stories of Saul and David as Theological Allegory." *Vetus Testamentum* 50, 4 (2000): 519–30.

Sanford, John A. *King Saul, the Tragic Hero: A Study in Individuation.* New York: Paulist Press, 1985.

Seow, Choon-Leong. *The First and Second Books of Kings: Introduction, Commentary, and Reflections.* Vol. 3 of *The New Interpreter's Bible.* Nashville: Abingdon Press, 1999.

Steussy, Marti J. *David: Biblical Portraits of Power.* Columbia: University of South Carolina Press, 1999.

von Rad, Gerhard. *Holy War in Ancient Israel.* Trans. Marva J. Dawn. Grand Rapids: William B. Eerdmans, 1991.

Other books from The Pilgrim Press

KRAZY KINFOLK
Exploring Dysfunctional Families in the Bible

BARBARA J. ESSEX

0-8298- 1654-2/paper/128 pages/$16.00

Essex continues in the tradition of her popular Bible studies. Each study unit reviews the stories of selected biblical "dysfunctional" families such as: 1) Abraham, Sarah, and Hagar; 2) Jacob, Leah, and Rachel; 3) Moses, Miriam, and Aaron; 4) Lois, Eunice, and Timothy; 5) Mordecai and Esther; and 6) Mary, Martha, and Lazarus.

BAD BOYS OF THE NEW TESTAMENT
Exploring Men of Questionable Virtue

BARBARA J. ESSEX

0-8298-1672-0/paper/128 pages/$16.00

This seven-week small group study focuses on stories of selected biblical "bad boys" in the New Testament—stories such as the elder brother of the prodigal son parable, the Pharisees, Judas Iscariot, Pontius Pilate, and Ananias. A short commentary follows each scripture. Reflection questions conclude each unit, offering participants the opportunity to start a discussion about what can be learned from these characters and their stories.

BAD BOYS OF THE BIBLE
Exploring Men of Questionable Virtue

BARBARA J. ESSEX

0-8298-1466-3/paper/124/$14.00

Cain, Abraham, Adam, Samson, Lot, Jacob, and Jepthah are well-known men of the Bible who were strong and faithful, yet also weak and challenged. In this best-selling text, Essex takes readers on a journey to explore male giants of faith.

BAD GIRLS OF THE BIBLE
Exploring Women of Questionable Virtue

BARBARA J. ESSEX

0-8298-1339-X/paper/114 pages/$14.00

Designed as a fourteen-week study, this resource explores biblical accounts of traditionally misunderstood or despised women as they are presented in the Bible. Reflection questions are included, as well as suggestions for preaching and teaching.

IN SEARCH OF FAITH
Profiles of Biblical Seekers

HOWARD W. ROBERTS

0-8298-1412-4/paper/176 pages/$12.00

This resource explores biblical characters who struggled to define their faith lives. It is designed to help readers identify with biblical characters, discover kinship with seekers of another era, and read about themselves in these stories. It can be used for small study groups and as a sermon series.

To order these or any other books from THE PILGRIM PRESS call or write to:

THE PILGRIM PRESS
700 PROSPECT AVENUE EAST
CLEVELAND, OHIO 44115-1100

Phone orders: 1-800-537-3394
Fax orders: 216-736-2206

Please include shipping charges of $5.00 for the first book and $0.75 for each additional book.

Or order from our web sites at www.pilgrimpress.com and www.ucpress.com.

Prices subject to change without notice.